Sandra Boston

Aim Your Mind

Strategies and skills for
conscious communication

**CONSCIOUS
COMMUNICATION**
INSTITUTE

GREENFIELD, MASSACHUSETTS

SYLLABUS FOR BASIC SKILLS

CLASS 1: Cultural Patterns as Barriers to Conscious Communication

We will look at our present conflict styles when encountering trouble, and the influence of culture and family of origin on our habits of unconscious communication. We will explore barriers to conscious communication and the underlying values that motivate our behavior in conflict.

CLASS 2: When Someone Else Is Upset: Active Listening

We explore a roadmap for moving from unconscious to conscious communication. Learning the Active Listening skill allows us to be actively involved in helping another who is upset, while remaining separate from their problem and avoiding unconscious cultural habits of "helping". We support them to be the best solver of their problem.

CLASS 3: When We Are Upset: I-Message

We often avoid conflict as long as we can because of our very real fear that bringing it up will make things worse. If we have a positive attitude toward conflict—that it is healthy and necessary in any relationship—and we also feel skillful about introducing it, relationships will feel safer and improve with the flow of information.

CLASS 4: Navigating Differences in Relationships: Taking the Heat

The other person is going to react to our I-Message. We learn to expect this and know what to do to create a nonviolent interaction. We reflect feelings and name needs in order to create the safety and cooperation needed to stay in the interaction and continue to explore differences. Then we can move on to negotiation. Because conflict is triggering, we learn to watch our own internal communication, maintain our intent to learn, and support ourselves and the other to stand our ground.

CLASS 5: Negotiation: Sharing Power in Deciding What Happens Next

Since the whole process of conflict happens when someone needs change, resolution can only happen when the others involved have been persuaded to cooperate with that change. Resolution involves acknowledging how that change will impact them and what needs of theirs must therefore be part of the process of change.

CLASS 6: Unresolved Conflict: Managing Values Differences

Learning the skills of serenity, respecting differences and, as Scott Peck says, "Protecting each other's solitude" are great challenges to our desire to be in control. How do we *gracefully* hear a "No" to what we would like, elevate our needs to preferences, and extend our personal support system so we always have options?

CLASS 7: Putting It All Together: Skills, Strategies, and Personal Victory

Many of the skills we use in values differences are skills for our relationship with ourselves. We have to stand our ground with what matters most to us, while taking the heat of differences gracefully. Our victory is not dependent upon the outcome, but in how we conduct ourselves. We explore how freedom relates to loving, requiring our highest degree of personal commitment, stamina and intention to honor separateness.

CLASS 8: Taking a Non-Negotiable Stand, Evaluation, Graduation

Sometimes a value, a prior agreement, a role with obligations to a third part, or an overwhelming need cause us to reach a bottom line. We are not willing to negotiate what will happen next. There may be strong negative consequences for those affected by our choice. We learn how to minimize this negative effect on the relationship.

CONTENTS

The content of each chapter parallels the curriculum of the eight week training
in Basic Skills for Conscious Communication.

CONSCIOUS COMMUNICATION
INSTITUTE

Greenfield, Massachusetts
Founded by Sandra Boston, 2000

"How we communicate shapes the course of our lives." — Sandra Boston

Mission Statement:

To help individuals, families, organizations and communities to create healthy lives.

To model, teach and supervise others to use skills and strategies that maximize the possibility of resolving differences in ways that improve relationships and empower all those involved.

To create a culture with a positive regard for differences as an opportunity to learn, to love, and to grow.

LONG-DISTANCE LEARNING PROGRAM

The program includes three conference calls with the participant and a buddy for the purpose of practicing the skills with coaching; this text book (the student version); and the audio tapes of the eight classes taught by Sandra Boston which are available on the website. It also includes one hour of personal counseling on how to apply the skills being taught to a particular personal situation. On-going counseling is available for a fee.

For information on this program, visit our website
www.ccitraining.org
or contact Sandra Boston 413-774-5952, Bostons111@gmail.com

DEDICATION

To my three sons

*Aaron, who at the very beginning, when he was just four,
would remind me to take a penny out of the jar on the kitchen table
if I forgot to use my skills and yelled at him.*

*Nathan, who, whenever I would frantically start owning his problem,
would respond in his Buddha nature with, "Don't worry about it, Mom."*

*Kyle, who at twenty-three, took the risk of enrolling in this course
as part of his first professional training.*

ACKNOWLEDGMENTS

*Among those who taught me how to hold differences and stand my ground were George Lakey,
George and Lillian Willoughby, and many others from the Movement for a New Society
community in Philadelphia from 1970 to 1982. This community, one hundred and twenty strong,
conducted an international nonviolence training center for social change activists where I first
taught this course as "The Language of Nonviolence." Gandhi's principles and strategies were
integral to our work and I found many parallels between the political and personal application of
those strategies. Marshall Rosenberg was an important teacher for our community and much of
his model of nonviolent communication is integrated into this course. Also fundamental to my
growth were teachers from the Re-evaluation Co-counseling community- Keith and Kathy Miller
and Chuck Esser. Thomas Gordon, creator of Parent Effectiveness Training, (and his teacher
Carl Rogers) set me on the path to becoming a teacher of these skills. Arnold Mindell showed me
how to take these skills to the arena of the global community with its "sitting in the fire"
diversity issues and Margaret Paul ("Inner Bonding") showed me how to take the skills within.*

*I want to thank my owl-spirited editor, Gaella Elwell, for her extraordinary generosity of time
and care to complete this book. She brought her very patient, steadfast attention to details,
flavorful turn of sentence, and visual delight. We have made good use of the very skills we seek to
teach as we have honed our collaboration on CCI publications over four years. Gaella, you have
been a consistent model of the intent to learn and I am deeply grateful. I was also generously
assisted by two professional editors, Bruce Boston of Wordsmith, Inc. (Reston, Va.) and Beth
Berry of U.Mass Amherst. Thanks to Sunny Miller of Traprock Peace Center (Deerfield, Ma.) for
the hand-drawn illustrations.*

*Finally, I want to thank all those who have said "yes" to this course over the thirty years I have
taught it; who showed up each week, worked to integrate these skills into their lives, and brought
me stories that made my heart sing. And greatest kudos to those brave souls who have joined the
CCI teacher training and made the commitment to teach these skills to others. And so the river
flows on....*

CONSCIOUS COMMUNICATION TOOLBOX

CENTERING
SELF-TALK

p. 24-8

"Oh," Breathe, "Wow"
Welcome my imperfections
Don't catch the ball
Bring my behavior to choice (scale of 1-10)

CONSCIOUS COMMUNICATION ROADMAP

p.29-40

Who needs change?
How am I *feeling* about what is happening?

ACTIVE LISTENING

p.32-38

Other Person is upset; they need change.
I accept what they are feeling.
Focus on their feelings, use my empathy

I-MESSAGE

p.43ff

I am upset; I want change.
Key Phrases to introduce my needs
Reverse I-Message to field attacks

STANDING MY GROUND: Self-talk to:

p.71ff

Maintain my personal boundary
Manage my anxiety, take the heat
Separate feelings from thinking

NEGOTIATING

p.83ff

Data-based problem; we both want change
Frame problem as needs and feelings, the "dance"
Share power in deciding what happens
Personal victory

EXPLORING VALUES

p.97ff

Opinion-based problem: other doesn't need change
Curious - "That's interesting, tell me why…"
"I /we see it differently."
True vs. inherited values
Hold two points of view

NON-NEGOTIABLE STAND

p.123-6

Accountable for negative consequences to relationship
Restore power where possible
My truth, not the truth

"In the end, all we have with each other is a relationship." Thomas Gordon

PREFACE

When I took Parent Effectiveness Training as a young parent, little did I know that I was entering into what would become my life work. Gregg Levoy, in *Callings: Finding and Following the Authentic Life,* asks the question: "What is it you were born to understand?" Now, twenty-nine years later, I can answer his question this way: *my calling is about how to create understanding when differences arise in important relationships, and how to share power in deciding what happens.* This is no small undertaking, particularly in a culture where domination and control are valued when conflict arises. I have been mightily supported by voices that have shared this calling throughout every century of human existence, from Lao Tzu, to Gandhi, to Thich Nhat Hanh. It is for the brave of heart. It is a High Dream. It calls us to expand our humanity and journey into the authentic life.

As with any High Dream, the more we strive, the more our shadow appears, teaching us that we dwell somewhere between heaven and earth. Teaching this course has given me great opportunities to laugh at myself and to welcome my imperfections, while never succumbing to the cynicism that the skills don't work. They do work—like the laws of nature. It is we who break against them: giving up, losing it, or blaming someone else. When this happens, we can find ourselves in the familiar pattern of needing to be right. I have had to learn to replace that need with what Gandhi called "experiments with truth," the willingness to listen and to be persuaded by how the other is experiencing what is happening. In welcoming my imperfections, I can choose to be a learner, a beginner, someone willing to go back and do an interaction over again if it doesn't go well. I find great freedom in no longer needing to be right about anything! One of my favorite teachers, Marshall Rosenberg, said, "Anything worth doing is worth doing poorly." His compassion supports all of us to press on, bringing a spirit of inquiry and humility to difficult interactions.

These skills have also supported me in healing my deepest self-esteem wounds. Learning to stand my ground, to stay connected to my own goodness and my intent to understand when I am under attack, has been the greatest laboratory for transforming my fear of unworthiness. It has taught me the power of loving myself, even in the midst of my imperfections or when someone else is trying to shame me into collapsing. Verbal attacks have become opportunities for me to ground myself and to bring my behavior to choice. Each encounter reminds me of someone going to the gym and picking up heavier weights than they used the week before. It is a healthy challenge. I have even been accused of liking conflict! One of my graduates said, "Once I realized the conflict wasn't about my self worth, my anxiety was gone and I could be in any conflict." That kind of breakthrough is what has kept me coming back to these skills year after year as the most important work I can be doing.

Another awareness that has come through years of teaching is differentiating personal victory from successful outcome of a conflict. Many conflicts involve long-held values that are not open to persuasion. A major part of our identity is rooted in what arouses passion in us. When we find ourselves embroiled in a conflict of values, our victory is not going to be in persuading the other to change, but in how we conduct ourselves. Here the skills give us a clear direction and strategy for how to proceed, so that our focus is not on getting the change we want, but on how we are creating understanding and building relationship with the other person. Gandhi defined conflict as the art of persuasion. We are practicing the art of human relationship. We may often fall short of the desired outcome, yet we can still feel grounded and successful as people who are making a difference on this planet, one interaction at a time. It has been said that the highest form of human intelligence is to observe without judging. The skills presented in this book support that ability. They teach us to hold the other person's best interest at heart, while also supporting our own interests. We have the tools to be as effective and influential as we can be. I call this Conscious Communication.

As we begin this journey together, let us pause to acknowledge all of our teachers, those who have inspired us by their example, and have put their wisdom into words that can be shared across time. Here we are, willing to take up the invitation to extend these skills into the future. Thank you for showing up. I welcome your passion, your energy, your creativity, your persistence, and your special gifts. Your contribution will enrich our collective endeavor and the culture that, together, we have the opportunity to transform.

At all new beginnings, I turn to Rumi for his compassionate guidance:

> Come, come, come, come,
> Wanderer, worshiper, lover of leaving,
> It does not matter.
> Ours is not a caravan of despair.
> Come, though you have broken your vows
> a thousand times,
> Come, yet again, come, come.

Sandra Boston de Sylvia
Greenfield, Massachusetts
January, 2005

ONE

CULTURAL PATTERNS
AND COMMUNICATION

We will look at our present communication styles, and how cultural and family dynamics have impacted our effectiveness when trouble arises. We will explore typical habits that limit our effectiveness, and identify the values and strategies that will nurture mutually respectful and empowering relationships.

Why is conflict so scary?

What outcome would I like to create as I deal with trouble?

Aiming Your Mind

Ours has been called the most violent culture in the world, with the highest homicide rate and the largest prison population, yet we market violence to every age group in our society beginning with Saturday morning cartoons. We have domestic violence in every socio-economic group and an escalating divorce rate in more than 50% of marriages. Our children are awash in a chain of family re-arrangements that leave them wondering just who their family is. We are losing our ability to live in harmony with nature— the only true economist—leaving less and less for future generations. This, too, is violence. Class warfare continues rewarding corrupt CEOs and punishing Moms and Pops. Who are we? Einstein warned that our moral development would be outpaced by our technological development. The UN is straining to maintain its mandate to build global consensus against the force of our go-it-alone foreign policy. It's time for us to face that our culture is based on the values of dominance and control and the use of power for our own gain without regard for the needs of others. Many nations see us as an arrogant, self-absorbed teenager with more money to spend than is good for us, and with no parental controls. No wonder we can't figure out how to parent our own teenagers. They mirror our deepest and most disturbing cultural values.

These social realities are painful to acknowledge, but that is our assignment. How does this relate to communication skills? Language is embedded in culture. When we begin to address the way we talk to one another when we have differences, we immediately feel fear of what will happen next. There are no talking sticks being passed around —as there are in indigenous cultures—so everyone has a chance to be heard. When in conflict with another, we risk judgment, insult, denial of our reality, and abandonment. The power to decide what happens resides in the one with the most control. This is oppression. Oppression creates marginalized people who become terrorists. Terrorists retaliate, and the dance of dominance and control goes on.

Our assignment…breathe…is to create a new culture, one in which we will raise our children to be safe, respected, and free from fear of others' judgments or control because they will know that they matter. How do we get there from here?

Someone once said to me, "Sandra, this course is about so much more than just communication skills." Yes, it *has* to be, because we can't change culture just by changing how we talk to one another. At the same time, we have to change the cultural beliefs and values that structure the ways we talk to one another, especially when there is conflict. This change is going to demand a powerful mix of vision, intention, skill, focus and courage.

> **Vision is the desired outcome.** A culture that respects differences is willing to hold each person's best interest at heart, believes that each one has a piece of the truth, and uses conflict creatively to meet the most needs possible.
>
> **Intention** is our commitment to live that vision in our daily interactions.
>
> **Skill** is how we will embody our intention and create our vision.
>
> **Focus and awareness** show our willingness to be about our assignment, not on automatic pilot asleep in the habits of culture.
>
> **Courage** is the fire in our belly that it will take to match the heat of change as the old resists the new.

When we begin to use the new skills, we will feel fear. It is not just the fear of the unfamiliar; it is the fear that these skills will not protect us. They don't fit with the dance of domination. We are going to have to let go of the ways we have protected ourselves–by hiding or attacking–as we make room for the new. We will feel this change in our bodies; we will feel anxious as we break patterns in ourselves and encounter resistance in others. When we change our relationship to conflict, and begin to see it as an opportunity to create understanding instead of needing to control the outcome, we will know that our cultural beliefs and values are changing.

I believe the greatest skill we have to manifest these changes is our ability to aim our mind.

 I believe the greatest skill we have to manifest these changes is our ability to aim our mind. We know about the cycle of abuse, and how those who abuse have transformed their habit of rage and violence—with the support of others—by taking responsibility for their anger and redirecting their energy into behaviors that don't hurt others. They learn to aim their mind toward their goal, to muster their intention and focus. Their courage is in being accountable to themselves and others. It is the courage of humility. As they transform themselves, they affect the values, attitudes, and behaviors of those around them. Domestic violence— once tacitly accepted—becomes less acceptable or tolerated. New expectations give rise to new institutions that reinforce the new values and behaviors. What was once a private matter behind closed doors is now a public responsibility. When people aim their mind and change themselves, institutions change, then culture changes.

Those who have overcome addictions through the guidance of the Twelve Step programs (again, within a supportive community) also learned to aim their mind toward serenity and walk the path of accountability with great courage and humility. Aiming the mind also has the power to dissolve tumors. It has the power, when practiced nonviolently by large numbers of people, as nonviolence, to topple empires. Surely we, too, can aim our mind to face into the fear of conflict with an intention to transform it from a mean-spirited competition for control into a meeting of human hearts who want the best for everyone involved.

When people aim their mind and change themselves, institutions change, then culture changes.

What we have learned from communities that have taken on the task of cultural transformation is that we, too, can do it-- one day at a time, one interaction at a time. We can't heal our culture until we first heal the disconnections within ourselves—the ways we have learned to separate from our goodness, our innocence, and our worthiness. As we reach for the skills of conscious communication, we also will encounter our fear of conflict, and our deeper fears about who we are. But these skills will point us toward healing. They affirm that we matter, and that our needs are important and deserving of our showing up to represent them in the heat of differences. We will meet conflict with our skillful vulnerability, and help each other to keep taking the steps necessary to transform our relationship with ourselves, with others, and ultimately with our culture. Alone, we are overwhelmed; together, we are powerful. All we have to do is aim our mind and stay connected with each other. This is how culture changes.

> Step by step, the longest march can be won, can be won
> Many stones do form an arch, singly none, singly none
> And by union what we will, can be accomplished still
> Drops of water turn the mill, singly none, singly none.
>   - United Mine Workers song

Does How We Communicate Shape the Course of Our Lives?

- Are you someone whose emotions run your life?

- When you are triggered, do you go out of control and stampede like a bull in a china shop?

- Are you so afraid of your emotions that you shut down when they are arising, go blank, get confused, or don't even know how to tell someone what you are feeling?

These behaviors have enormous consequences for our partners, and for those we work with, live with, or share other significant connections. They aren't going to understand us. They aren't going to feel understood, respected or supported by us. They will feel unsafe, insecure and "walking on egg shells" around us. Or they may even give up and leave us.

These consequences shape the course of our lives. They have profound effects on children, too, who are shaping their personalities through their relationship with us. How many people are miserable at work because there is someone they can't get along with? Do you have a relative you are not on speaking terms with, either because you feel terrified or hopeless about getting through to them? Do you wish you knew what to do— how to stand your ground— without reaping a whirlwind or submitting to an icy stare? It's time we recognize the importance of communication and become experts at it!

"It's Just a Little Trouble"

In graduate school, I came upon a book with a one-word title: *Trouble*. The author talked about how we spend so much of our life energy trying to avoid trouble, that when it

does come it seems like a catastrophe, a huge failure. Where did this cultural message come from? Who has ever been able to avoid trouble? How would our life be different if we saw trouble as normal and ordinary? If we planned for it, and were prepared for it, then it would be "just a little trouble." This phrase has become a familiar refrain among graduates of this course. "We had a little trouble, but we handled it OK." An outdoor instructor once told me, "There's no such thing as bad weather, only inappropriate clothing." That is the attitude we want to cultivate toward trouble—relaxed, accepting, and prepared for whatever comes.

Unfortunately, because of a superficial, judgmental attitude toward trouble, we are not trained and prepared to handle it. As a result, we meet it with confusion, irritation, and fear. Deep injuries from this lack of skill are passed on from generation to generation, with much suffering and perpetuation of abuse as a result. We don't allow people to drive cars without accountability to the fundamental rules necessary to make the highways safe for everyone. How we talk to each other can be just as important to our well-being as how we drive our cars; yet, as a culture, we do not learn even basic skills for how to communicate effectively.

With some basic understanding of cause and effect, and some useful skills and strategies for how to handle differences when they heat up, we can create more understanding and use conflict to improve relationships rather than destroy them. We can learn to:

- Listen and respond rather than react.

- Have a positive regard for differences and take the heat of exploring them.

- Cooperate rather than argue when we have to make difficult decisions.

A simple little argument can arise over whether to leave the back door propped open to catch a breeze, or to close it to prevent flies from coming in. It can either blow up into a mountain, or shrink into a molehill, depending on whether we listen and respond, or react and control. A little skill and training make all the difference.

What is Communication?

This may seem like a simple question. Most people would say it is listening while another is talking, or putting your thoughts into words. For me, it is a process of *creating understanding*. Sometimes we repeat back what someone has said, and they know we heard them, but that is not the same as the experience of being *understood*. They want to know that we received the *meaning* they intended, not just the content. It is when we feed back how we sense they are *feeling* that a circuit is completed, and they feel understood. To do this, we need awareness of our own feelings, and of the very process of communication itself, neither of which our culture readily provides. One graduate said:

> *"Listening has to be taught. I didn't realize I was just hearing and not listening until I learned how much goes into it. It is actually hard. It requires more self-awareness of my own feelings than I've ever had before."*

Communication is—at its core—about our most important needs, and the feelings generated by those needs. Yet our culture teaches us that boys shouldn't feel scared and girls shouldn't feel angry. We are shamed for our most vulnerable feelings and cut off from the very source necessary to create understanding.

"I Don't Want to Talk About It!"—A Culture of Control

Since conflict has such a bad reputation, and our mission is to change that, let's look below the surface and see what it really is. Our culture might be called the "Culture of Control," because, when dealing with trouble, so much of our behavior is defensive.

- We deny conflict: "I'm not angry."

- Avoid it: "I don't want to talk about it."

- Lie about it: "That's not what I said!"

- Punish and shame it: "Go to your room for talking back to your mother, you bad girl!"

We do these things in order to *maintain some semblance of control*. We play the "right/wrong game." If you disagree with me, then someone is right and someone is wrong. Conflict becomes a power struggle for control, which equates to being right. "Right" then becomes a by-product not of truth, but of the power to control an outcome.

This dynamic is what underlies all oppression. A powerful group negates the needs and feelings of a less powerful group, and uses the forces of control such as laws, police, army, prison, or denial of access to information and opportunity to reinforce their control. When those on either side of the power struggle adapt to this system, they fall into the learned habits of oppression, such as being silent, being nice, being depressed, being a rebel/criminal, and being addicted to substances that soothe the pain of powerlessness and denial of their reality. Unfortunately, these same habits serve to reinforce the system of control. We want to make an intervention in this culture of control, and bring the awareness and courage necessary to stand our ground without

For some, learning to share power will mean claiming power they have never felt they had before. For others, it will feel like giving up power because they realize they were previously using it to control others.

CULTURE OF CONTROL

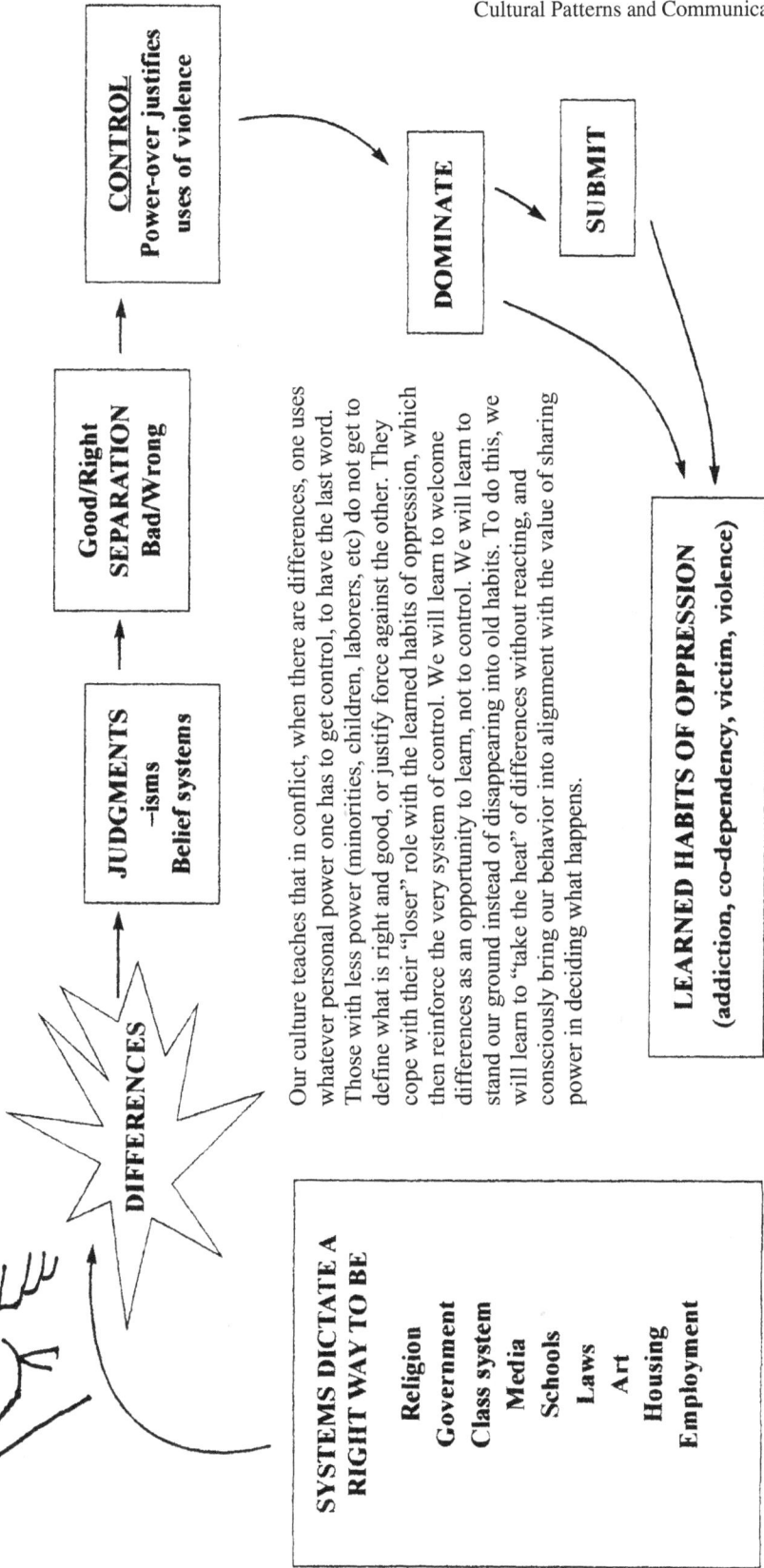

CONTROL
Power-over justifies uses of violence

DOMINATE

SUBMIT

Good/Right SEPARATION Bad/Wrong

**JUDGMENTS
–isms
Belief systems**

DIFFERENCES

Our culture teaches that in conflict, when there are differences, one uses whatever personal power one has to get control, to have the last word. Those with less power (minorities, children, laborers, etc) do not get to define what is right and good, or justify force against the other. They cope with their "loser" role with the learned habits of oppression, which then reinforce the very system of control. We will learn to welcome differences as an opportunity to learn, not to control. We will learn to stand our ground instead of disappearing into old habits. To do this, we will learn to "take the heat" of differences without reacting, and consciously bring our behavior into alignment with the value of sharing power in deciding what happens.

LEARNED HABITS OF OPPRESSION
(addiction, co-dependency, victim, violence)

SYSTEMS DICTATE A RIGHT WAY TO BE

Religion
Government
Class system
Media
Schools
Laws
Art
Housing
Employment

cooperating with being excluded or oppressed. We also want to be mindful of ways in which we may belong to a group that has more rank and may unwittingly be denying the rights and power of another group.

White women, in their struggle for equality with men, often are oblivious to how they are oppressing women of color in the way they go about their holding of personal power. Parents who feel oppressed in their workplace may be oblivious to how they are oppressing their children at home. There is a great deal to understand about power, and the new paradigm requires that we learn how to share power in deciding what happens. For some, this will mean claiming power they have never felt they had before; for others, it will feel like giving up power because they realize they were previously using it to control others rather than sharing it. The new culture requires us to change our whole relationship to power. It is a big assignment.

Who Has the Power?

Conflict is not about who is right or wrong. It is about important unmet needs.

I define having power as "the ability to decide what happens." When one person has more power—and that is usually the case—our cultural value of "might makes right" validates her right to control the situation. Parents control children, teachers control students, bosses control employees, and that's just the way it is. Actually, conflict is not about who is right or wrong. It is about unmet needs. It is about *important unmet needs.* We attempt to meet them with our personal power. When we bump into someone who has a problem with our behavior, the power struggle starts for who will decide what is going to happen next. We want to learn how to outsmart those habitual patterns of vying for winner and loser, and learn skills for addressing the needs below the conflict so we can cooperate in resolving them.

Getting to the Bottom of Culture and Conflict

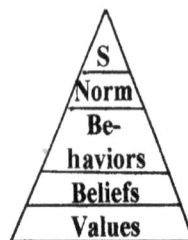

If we hope to change the way we approach conflict, then we need a deeper understanding of where it originates. Our judgments about right and wrong quickly heat up our blood pressure and create arguments. But they spring from beliefs that may be outside our awareness in the moment. These beliefs are in turn predicated on values. Now we are down in the core of what culture is: values, beliefs, behaviors, norms, and sanctions. We may be aware of what we are saying (though often not until after we have said it), but we are usually not aware of *why.*

It takes *consciousness* and *curiosity* to look beneath our "take" on things to uncover the beliefs and values that are generating our needs and feelings, and thus our behavior. We cannot just change our communication habits and hope for significant cultural change. We have to dig for the values and beliefs involved in our differences. We have to identify our inherited underlying values about power and conflict, and what values we would like to put in their place:

CULTURAL PARADIGM SHIFT

Present Cultural Value
Those with the most power have the right to make and enforce rules: win/lose

New Value
Sharing power in deciding what happens creates the best, lasting solution: win/win

Present Cultural Belief
Might makes Right
People in control are entitled to punish those who disagree with them
Parents know what's best for kids

New Belief
Meeting the most needs creates the best possibility of healthy relationships
Kid's needs are important, too

Present Behavior in Conflict
Be the boss, order and direct others
Impatient and demanding when upset
Need to be right and win in a conflict
Intent to protect: dominance is priority

New behavior in Conflict
Listen, identify needs, negotiate
Patient and curious
Resistance is information
Intent to learn: relationship is priority

Current cultural values teach that because I am older, or I am your boss, that I know what is best for you. That belief justifies my telling you what to do and enforcing my dictates with punishment if necessary. If, on the other hand, I value respecting differences and sharing power, I will choose to negotiate mutually respectful solutions to our differences regardless of differences of rank.

We have to respect how slowly any culture changes. As we begin to learn new communication skills, which are predicated on a new value system, we will meet resistance—big time. We will hear things like, *"That's a bunch of crap!" "That doesn't work." "Don't talk to me weird like that."* We will have to be able to take the "heat" of change. We will need the company of others who also want to create change in how we handle trouble and conflict. We will need to deeply understand what we are taking on, and trust the process of change. Any system will resist change; that is a normal, and an important part of the process of persuasion. If people resist, they are also engaged, even if defensively.

How would a shift in values affect our communication patterns? What would accountability in communication look like if we valued relationship over dominance?

- How would our lives be different if, from the age of three, we were taught basic skills for standing our ground, or for listening beneath anger and criticism to the underlying messages of need and desire?

- How would it be different if, when trouble arose, we felt safe because we knew what to do?

- How would it be different if we understood how to help other people when we saw they were in conflict?

- How would it be different if conflict were treated as a normal occurrence requiring awareness and process to resolve, and not as something that inevitably creates winners and losers?

React or Respond: Styles of Handling Conflict

What do you do when you say to your child: *"Come on, we have to go now,"* and the response is, *"I don't want to!"* You tell your partner you want to spend more time together and he complains that you want too much? Your boss is impatient with you when you have worked overtime to help him out? If you react–act without thinking–you will fall into your habitual way of handling the tension of conflict. If you have skills, you can *think* about what is happening, *evaluate* your options, and *choose* your response.

When the less powerful turn into "losers", they habitually either rebel or submit. That makes them either bad or good in the eyes of the controllers. This judgment is reinforced both by multigenerational role-models and sanctions in the family that shame the rebellious and reward the obedient. John Bradshaw, in *The Family: A Revolutionary Way to Self-Discovery,* describes how these two defenses then become a central part of our personalities, creating either:

- **Internalizers** – the obedient ones, who fear being abandoned, so avoid conflict, give in, and are seen as good, or

- **Externalizers** – the rebels, who fear being controlled, so fight back, attack, push the other away, and are seen as bad.

Both of these styles of conflict are adaptations to the old models of power and control. Both people are feeling anxious because their basic needs to either belong or be independent are being threatened. They are both acting to alleviate their anxiety, though for different reasons. They are not choosing their behavior, but automatically reacting to their own desperate feelings and their fear of losing.

Internalizers seem to lose, and Externalizers seem to win. Our culture doesn't provide any other role models for how to behave when trouble arises. People are afraid of conflict because they are expecting to win or lose, and most fear losing because that was their predominant experience as a child. Internalizers handle conflict by withdrawing, agreeing to lose and forfeiting their needs in order to get relief from the "heat" of the conflict, but they feel lonely and invisible. Externalizers pressure until they "win," but they experience disconnection and isolation. So which one really wins? Winning is a myth which enchants our culture but which brings no lasting peace or satisfaction.

Winning is a myth which enchants our culture but which brings no lasting peace or satisfaction.

In *The Conscious Heart,* Gay and Kathryn Hendricks elaborate further on our coping styles by describing four patterns of reaction. They call these the four *expressions of fear:*

Fight: By *fighters*, they mean shouters who are using anger as a weapon.

Flee: Those who *flee* will slam doors, stay late at the office, sulk, and play hard to get.

Freeze: *Freezers* are immobilized by conflict. They try to become invisible and can't think of anything to say.

Faint: *Fainters* space out, fog over until the danger passes; they are out of their bodies, and nothing makes any sense to them.

None of these behaviors support a process which can lead to a resolution acceptable to all parties. They all reinforce the win/lose dynamic. They become a rigid part of our personality, which eventually we may feel helpless to change. Our reaction to conflict is then automatic, so we get the same results every time it happens. We begin to believe "Conflict never solves anything." We don't feel that we have any choice or can make any difference in what happens when we or the other person get upset. We want to overcome these habits of self-protection, by learning skills that support us to alleviate our anxiety, tolerate differences, stay engaged and resolve differences. The real challenge comes when our intellect ("I see a better way") collides with these deeply engrained personality structures, which are much harder to change than ideas. Now we can see why this change we are seeking is so demanding. Before we can use our new skills, we have to confront and

Before we can use our new skills, we have to confront and change deep-seated beliefs about ourselves.

change deep-seated beliefs about ourselves, from " I am less important, or my needs are less important" to "My needs matter and so do yours."

"What's Really Going On?"—The Infrastructure of Conflict

Judgments of right and wrong trigger competing coping behaviors. What other responses to conflict can there be? If we take the judgments away, what we have are *different needs*. Two fundamental needs are operating in any important relationship:

- Our need to express our independence
- Our need to belong.

We are always expressing our need for independence, autonomy, and spontaneous self-expression through our behavior. This is the source of our uniqueness and individuality. Our autonomy is a problem only if it comes into conflict with someone else's need for the same.

Now a new dynamic is introduced—the relationship. When it is not a significant relationship, we tend to disregard the discomfort of the differences, but when *our need to belong* is involved, we are now in a quandary. Pursuing our solutions upsets the other person's autonomy, and they object. They try to get us to stop doing what we are doing. It *looks* like we have competing solutions, but what we actually have is conflict of our need for independence and our need to belong. *This dynamic is the essence of conflict.*

Internalizers are wedded to their need to belong and forfeit their need for independence to alleviate their anxiety and end the conflict.

Externalizers are wedded to their need for independence, and forfeit their need to belong in order to alleviate their anxiety and end the conflict.

We want to see conflict as an opportunity to learn more about each other, and even improve our relationship.

Neither one is capable of *resolving* the conflict, because they are too busy protecting their own dominant needs. They have been trained by the culture to believe that they have to choose; there is no way to have differences, and represent their needs in a way that protects their connection. We want to find a process that allows for both of these important needs to be respected, not negated. We want to make an intervention in this "Culture of Control," by changing our *attitude toward conflict.* Instead of seeing it as bad, dangerous, hurtful, and "making things worse," we want to see it as an opportunity to learn more about each other, and even improve our relationships by honoring the two fundamental needs in each person. We want to eliminate forcing either party to choose between these needs. It would sound something like this:

> Parent: *"Come on, we have to go now!"*
>
> Child: *"I don't want to go!"*
>
> Parent: *"I can see this is upsetting to you. Help me understand why it's so important to you to keep doing what you are doing."*
>
> Child: *"Billy and I haven't finished our game. It's not fair!"*
>
> Parent: *"So it's important to you not to be interrupted until you finish your game."*
>
> Child: *"Yeah."*
>
> Parent: *"How about if I give you five more minutes?"*
>
> Child: *"OK. Let's hurry up, Billy!"*

The parent needs to accomplish a task that requires leaving the house. The child needs to finish his game with his friend. We want a positive regard for this process of discovering different needs–a way that takes patience and curiosity. We want to feel skillful and confident and to communicate in a way that does not ask the other person to choose between her autonomy and her need to belong. We want to be able to have an honest difference of needs without activating defenses, honoring the *whole* person in each of us—with our autonomy *and* our need to belong—when there is "just a little trouble."

"Shame On You!"

One of the more powerful forces used to get us to separate from our own self-interest is to shame us for wanting what we want. We grew up hearing:

> *"How many times do I have to tell you not to leave dirty dishes in the living room!"*
>
> *"You're impossible!"*
>
> *"All you care about is yourself."*

The message behind these words, and behind all shaming is, *"You are bad for wanting what you want."* This is one of the most powerful methods of social control, cloaked in terms of "teaching a child to behave." Of course, this only works to control us when we feel vulnerable with the person who is doing the shaming. It is interesting to notice that shaming doesn't work if we don't care about the relationship involved. But, do we ever care when it is someone with whom we feel dependent or vulnerable! In *Undefended Love,* authors Psaris and Lyons mention that 33% of adults they worked with in one class were unable to even name their own needs anymore, as a result of the pain experienced around wanting something they could not get or were told was even wrong to want.

Shaming is powerful precisely because it threatens our two most basic needs. This generates intense anxiety, which causes us to immediately grab for a defense that will alleviate it. Here we meet the Externalizer who attacks to push the other away, and the Internalizer who withdraws. Both are doing the same thing – trying to end the conflict so the anxiety will subside. We call these defenses Protective Patterned Responses. They are learned from multi-generational family patterns. They become habitual and unconscious and then, because we are not aware of having any choice, we repeat them and pass them on to the next generation with no idea that there is something more effective to do. We are now caught in the automatic behavior of a dysfunctional will *("I wish I didn't lose my temper but I can't help it."),* and rigid patterns of winning and losing which leave us vulnerable to the next incident. *(See chart on page 16.)*

Sometimes the pain of this repetition is so intense we cover it over with addictions to soothe ourselves. The addictive substance is a replacement for what we really want because it is easier to get. In The Recovery Movement, it is taught that reclaiming our ability to "want what we want" is a sign of returning mental health. Recovery is a return to being willing to listen to ourselves and having the courage to make choices that are good for us, even if others are disturbed by what we choose. It is a healing journey, and one that would not need to happen if our needs were not squelched so early in our lives by shaming and the resulting fear of conflict.

It is a mystery why some children respond to shaming by rebelling, by firing their parent as an authority in their life, and staying connected to their own truth with so little external support. Most children buckle, separate from their authentic self in order to belong, and internalize the blow to their self-esteem that shaming causes. (*"If I want that, then I am bad. I do want that, so, I must be bad.") Conflict becomes associated with our self-worth.* When someone is angry with us, we then begin to automatically assume that we have done something wrong or bad. Now conflict has become about much more than just competing needs and solutions; it is about our core belief about our self-worth. We begin to dread conflict.

> *Recovery is a return to being willing to listen to ourselves and having the courage to make choices that are good for us even if others are disturbed by what we choose.*

The Goblins Within: Shame Attacks

Now we have a personality set in motion that may eventually become either a bad person (because that is what they believe they are), or someone obsessive about being good (in other people's eyes) so that their fear of being bad is never uncovered. These *false selves* will not be able to tell the truth in a conflict situation because we will be hit from within by a "shame attack." We will suffer *automatic, undesirable feelings of vulnerability—such as fear, anger or anxiety*—which will trigger our protective defenses. We will know we are having a shame attack because our body will be in turmoil. Our blood pressure will rise, our face flush, our palms sweat, our throat go dry, our eyes tear, or our head begin to throb. Our own internal shame attacks can be more devastating to our authentic self than anything someone else can say to us. When they are unexamined we react to defend so quickly that we don't even see that it is our own thoughts that are scaring us, thoughts like:

"If he is mad at me, I've done something wrong."

"I've frustrated her again. I'm just a failure. I don't deserve to be loved."

Most likely, we are not even aware that we are thinking these thoughts. We just feel the dread that is generated by them. When we react this way, we separate from our own needs in order to feel safe. What we *really feel, need, and want* are left in the dust. We end up with the familiar patterns of internalizer and externalizer as we attempt to manage our ensuing anxiety. (*See chart on Shame Attacks next page*)

To begin to undo this habitual reaction, we have to re-kindle our self-worth. We have to welcome our own imperfections, and tell ourselves we are lovable and capable. Then we are ready to work with our pain. We have to be able to tolerate the pain long enough to investigate the negative beliefs about our self that are the true source of our shame attack.

- Under my immediate fear of being abandoned, is going to be

- A fear that I am not worthy of love, because of

- A deeper belief that I am unlovable.

SHAME ATTACKS

Shaming is one of the most effective forms of social control. When used by a care-taker on a dependent person, both one's need for independence and one's need to belong are threatened. The anxiety generated creates an urgent need for defense. Repeated often enough, we internalize the shamer and shame ourselves when someone is upset with us.

EVENT

INDEPENDENCE IN ✱ CONFLICT WITH NEED TO BELONG

FEELING

FEEL OUT OF CONTROL

BEHAVIOR

SHAME → I'M NOT OK.

I FEEL SHAME when a parent acts in hurtful ways, SHAMELESSLY.

ANXIETY

ABANDONMENT (physical and emotional)

RAGE

PROTECTION/ PATTERNED RESPONSES

RESULTING FEELINGS ARE TOO PAINFUL OR SOCIALLY UNACCEPTABLE

INTERNALIZER
(victim in conflict)

- EFFECT IS HURT IN CONFLICT
- FEAR: BE ABANDONED
- SAD, LONELY IN CONFLICT
- MISTRUST OTHERS
- SEE SELF AS BAD IN CONFLICT

EXTERNALIZER
(dominator in conflict)

- EFFECT IS ANGER IN CONFLICT
- FEAR: BE TRAPPED/CONTROLLED
- RESENTMENT/BLAME IN CONFLICT
- MISTRUST OTHERS
- SEE OTHERS AS BAD IN CONFLICT

LEARNED HABITS OF OPPRESSION

- AUTOMATIC BEHAVIOR, DYSFUNCTIONAL WILL (can't choose), RIGID ROLES

Psaris and Lyons call this process of inquiry "the vertical drop" into the "black hole". They teach us to go into that pain rather than defend against it. Then we learn how to call in a compassionate part of our self who can bring caring and tenderness to our hurt self. When we are successful, our deepest fears about our self-worth can begin to dissolve. This internal work is essential to being able to confidently use the new communication skills.

After we do this deep inner work, when other people attempt to shame us it will be like someone trying to hang a coat on a hook that just isn't there. When our fears dissolve, we can hold onto our needs when they are different from another's, without judgment or shaming of either person. Then we can stay connected with the other person and learn to negotiate our differences and share power in deciding what happens next. One of my students put it this way:

> *"Just because someone is mad at me doesn't mean I've done anything wrong."*

The day I knew I was no longer vulnerable to shaming was when I realized that whether other people liked me or not was about them, and not about me. I realized that everyone is always finding what s/he is looking for. If they are looking for a reason not to like me, they will find it. If they are looking for a reason to like me, they will find it. Me, I'm just the same person doing whatever I'm doing. This was very liberating. I no longer had to figure out what someone else wanted and give it to them in order to be liked. I just had to be me, and be willing to accept that some people were not going to like me no matter what I do. I was no longer available for a shame attack. What a relief! One of my favorite teachers, Byron Katie, puts it this way, *"What someone else thinks about me is none of my business!"*

This is good news. If we had to change other people's words and behavior in order to feel safe, it would be hopeless. We don't have the power to do that; *"The door of change only opens from the inside"* (Stephen Covey). When <u>we</u> are the ones who have to change in order to avoid a shame attack, *that is good news*, because it is entirely possible for us to do that! Without skills, we will be stuck with the shame, only able to hide and defend, and not able to change what is happening. Being able to name a shame attack, know what is happening, and have choices about how to move through it and transform it, gives us hope that we can also transform how we handle conflict in our society. If we are no longer afraid of conflict because we aren't available for shaming, we can then learn how to use conflict to actually improve our relationships. *(See illustration next page.)*

"Just because someone is mad at me doesn't mean I've done anything wrong."

CONFLICT BEFORE OUR RESPONSE TO SHAMING IS HABITUAL

When there is no shaming,
we can stand our ground
(or our tricycles) and take
the heat.

CONFLICT AFTER OUR RESPONSE TO SHAMING IS HABITUAL

Compassion at the Core

Now we understand three main reasons why conflict is so scary:

- It represents an attack on our self-esteem (our sense of worthiness).

- It threatens our need to belong.

- It threatens our need for independence.

We are operating at the core of our sense of security! We may have internalized the belief that our needs were bad, or that they were the cause of the trouble. We may have learned to make our own needs disappear in order to belong. It is going to take a mighty force for change to reclaim those needs and give them a voice. We need a safe internal environment in order to do this. The resource we have with which to create this safety is compassion. Psaris and Lyons define compassion as being gentle, tender, and kind. It is only when we are being kind to ourselves—really listening, and acting to support ourselves without judgment—that we will have the inner calm to keep our hearts open to those with whom we are in conflict. With compassion for ourselves, we are freed from the "grip of our past," and we are safe, no matter what someone else may say or do. We are going to tell ourselves:

- *"I am good, even when I have made mistakes."*

- *"I am OK, even if someone is mad at me."*

- *"My needs are not bad; they are just in conflict with those of a significant other."*

- *"I'm not available for a shame attack!"*

"Let Me Tell You What To Do" - Barriers to Effective Communication

It is not surprising that we find our language reinforcing the underlying values of power and control.

Unfortunately, because of our cultural beliefs about what is "helpful" when someone is upset, we say things that mean well but fail to create understanding. In our eagerness, we "take charge" and direct the other person with advice, interpretations, analysis, and judgments instead of being present in a supportive way. How could it be that our very desire to be helpful could be delivering something hurtful? What could be hurtful about saying,

"I'm sure you'll feel better tomorrow."

"What did the teacher say to you?"

"I think you should just not think about it anymore, get over it."

As we patiently look below the surface of our conflict styles and ways of communicating, it is not surprising that we find our language reinforcing the underlying values of power and control. Let us look again at our cultural beliefs about trouble:

- If trouble is bad, then it has to be stopped.

- If trouble means something is out of control, then it has to be brought under control.

- If the other person isn't bringing it under control, then someone (namely we) should.

> *People simply want to be understood, even with their unsolved problems and negative feelings.*

With these beliefs, no wonder we think we have to do something when there is trouble! We are unaware that we are driven by these cultural beliefs to say things that are invalidating to the listener and that stop the flow of communication. When these same statements are directed to us, we feel our *own* discomfort. So underneath messages as seemingly helpful as giving advice, logical solutions, ordering, or directing we are also saying:

> **"Let me solve this problem, because obviously you don't know what to do and it <u>has</u> to be solved."**

Under our reassuring, sympathizing, interpreting, and questioning is the message:

> **"I'm upset by seeing you upset. Let me tell you what to do, so <u>I</u> can feel better."**

It is confusing to consider that such seemingly supportive comments as praising, agreeing, or reassuring are barriers to understanding. Aren't they caring, positive, and kind? In fact, they are all our attempts *to talk the person out of what they are really feeling.* If they were feeling positive about themselves, they wouldn't be upset. When we want to cheer them up, we have to examine our motives, notice our own discomfort, and own that we are really trying to make *ourselves* feel better. We are missing how much they simply want to be understood, even with their unsolved problems and negative feelings.

Probing questions are also barriers when asked to someone who is upset:

> *"Why did you say that?"*

> *"Why didn't you tell them you were..."*

> *"What did you say to her next?"*

Wanting more information may seem supportive; but ask yourself what you are going to do with the information when you get it. Your questioning indicates that you are starting to take charge of their problem. They will start feeling that it is being taken out of their hands, and maybe that you can do it better than they can. They may stop trying to solve it themselves, or start the endless "Yeah, but..." that goes nowhere. Questioning also structures an interaction. When we are asked a question, we are pulled out of our frame of reference and into that of the questioner. It separates us from our spontaneous internal process. It may satisfy the questioner's mind, but not the one who is in the dilemma. For example, someone who has just been fired is asked:

"Why didn't you stand up for yourself and tell him what you think?"

The person may not know the answer to that question, and besides, her mind is focused on what she is going to do now that she has been fired, not what she could have done differently. The question distracts her. It is really in service to the questioner, who is probably wondering why she didn't do what he would have done in that situation. The question just isn't helpful to the person with the dilemma.

It is usually surprising, and somewhat upsetting, for us to take a look at how we have used these directives as a way of handling trouble. We have believed that what we were doing was helpful. We have identified ourselves as caring, concerned supporters. We may be embarrassed when we look below the surface and recognize that: we are *acting to alleviate our own anxiety about trouble*, and we are doing it in socially acceptable ways. It just takes a simple flip of the coin—becoming recipients of these messages instead of senders—to feel their sting and our natural urge to block or withdraw from them. It is important to reiterate that these habitual responses to trouble are unsupportive only when the person we are "helping" is upset. There are many situations where ordering, lecturing or threatening are appropriate and helpful, such as when a child is playing in a dangerous situation. Asking good questions is supportive when the listener is available to go where the questions may lead.

Welcome to your humanity—you learned these habits of helping right along with your mother tongue. Welcome to your own openness to learning. Welcome to change, which will bring more trust, closeness, and sharing into your important relationships as you learn new ways of responding to someone who is upset. Now, when you see that someone you care about is upset, you will tell yourself "It's just a little trouble." Nothing needs to be fixed. I'm OK, and this person is going to solve this problem when they are ready in the way that is best for them. In Chapter Two, we will find out what to do *instead* of using these habits that will be helpful in truly supporting the other to discover her own solutions to her problems.

PUTTING IT INTO ACTION - 1

1. How do you define communication?

2. Where in the cycle of the Culture of Control do we want to make an intervention?

3. What is a shame attack? How do you know it is happening? What can you do about it?

4. If you are an Externalizer/Internalizer, what is your habitual response to conflict? What do you need to focus on to improve your communication? What will you find most challenging about that assignment?

5. What are the hidden messages in our typical ways of "helping" an upset person that stop communication?

TWO

THE MAP AND THE COMPASS
FOR CONSCIOUS COMMUNICATION

> *We will explore a roadmap for moving from unconscious to conscious communication. Learning the Active Listening skill allows us to be actively involved in helping another who is upset, while remaining separate from their problem and avoiding unconscious cultural habits of "helping". We support them to be the best solver of their problem.*

"The very act of listening to ourselves contradicts all the habits of oppression and protection we have adopted." – Sandra Boston

Intent to Learn or Intent to Protect

If we are in a situation where trouble arises, and we are not reaching for familiar defenses, we are going to learn something. If we want response-able relationships we have to be willing to be learners. We have to be willing to be changed.

When conflict is redefined by our new values, we ask not who is right or wrong, but what each person is needing and feeling.

This approach is not nearly as frightening as hoping our usual defenses will keep us safe. Our skills are going to point us in the direction of being *curious* instead of being right, but our *intention* to learn has to come first. That intention is grounded in our desire to change our values and beliefs about conflict and communication.

We choose to value mutual vulnerability and the importance of maintaining relationship when differences arise. We believe that respecting what each person needs and feels is the best way to reach our goal. The skills of conscious communication will give us the language to implement this shift from old values to new.

The Politics of "I Matter"

Margaret Paul, in *Inner Bonding*, teaches us how to be a responsible adult by relating empathically to our own inner child who is caught in all of the fears and protective patterns of childhood. She points us to the essential truth that to create change in our relationships with others, we have to begin with ourselves. If we are in reaction to what others are saying or doing, we are not free to listen to anyone. When we take the time to listen inwardly, we can transform our fear of shaming and losing. Then we can relate to others in empowering ways. So let's "unpack" this positive "self talk", and find out how important it is to first listen—with the intent to learn—to ourselves.

> *To create change in our relationships with others, we have to begin with ourselves.*

The very act of listening to ourselves contradicts all the habits of oppression and protection we have adopted. If we were not listened to as a child, we didn't learn to listen to ourselves. So the very first skill is one of *awareness,* of realizing we even have the *choice* to ask.

> ***"How am I feeling about what is happening? What do I need in this situation?"***

These may be the two most important questions we ask as we transition from the old culture to the new. If we ask with the old intent to protect, we will come up with what we *should* be feeling or needing in order to *control* the situation. If we ask with the intent to learn, we make space for our authentic selves to be heard. To do this, we have to also be prepared to take the heat that may follow. The skill that makes this opening for our true needs and feelings is conveyed in a tiny, two-letter word that I think has the power to not only change a culture, but to change the world. This word is *"Oh."*

How can this little word be so powerful? "Oh" represents choice; it represents the awareness that there is trouble, that we are having feelings about it, and we need to be careful—skillful—about what we do next.

> ***Those who cannot focus on their own inner process are destined to act out of past defensive behaviors, which can only perpetuate the cycles of power struggle.***

Being able to bring awareness and choice to what is happening is:

- Like shifting a car into neutral when you approach an intersection. It makes sense to stop and look both ways, not only for your own safety, but for that of others as well. Why not assume the same necessity when a difference arises in a relationship? Don't we want to have the same concern for our emotional safety and for that of the other?

- It's like noticing the red light on the dashboard of a car. It simply warns that trouble is brewing. If we pay attention, and take appropriate action, the trouble goes away. If we ignore it, it gets worse. Why not pay attention to it?

- The switch on a track that must be thrown if the train is to pull into the station. If the engineer ignores it, the train passes the station by and the connection is lost. That is what some people do with trouble—ignore it, go on by, and lose the connection.

When we can say "Oh," then all the new skills and strategies for how to handle trouble are available to us. If we can't do this, we are too quickly into the intersection or past the station and none of the skills matter at all. "Oh" is really about the skill of being a separate person who can observe what is happening without reacting. This separateness defies what our culture has defined as loving and caring when another person is upset. We are supposed to be upset, too. We are supposed to show our caring by immediately starting to problem-solve, or tell them what to do. It will feel very strange at first to resist these habitual responses. It may feel like we're not doing anything, and that will feel uncaring.

So I recommend saying "Oh" to someone or something at least five times a day for the next three weeks. Experts say that if we practice a new behavior for twenty-one days, it will become a habit. If you are serious about learning these skills and changing your relationship to conflict, try this experiment! It may be simple, but it isn't easy. *Old habits are going to be your greatest obstacle to gaining use of these skills.* How wonderful that the first step is so simple, and so powerful: Just say *"Oh."*

I have noticed that when I am upset, the word "Wow" spontaneously arises. It has now come to mean: *"I have some work to do here."* It wakes me up. Along with the consciousness of pausing, we can also take the space to breathe. Being aware of our breath not only slows us down, it puts us in the mode of both observing and participating. This is essential to being able to respond with skill instead of reacting to what is happening. If we are really upset, we will certainly be pulled back into our habits of protection, unless we first use our breath to ground us in our own goodness and in the relationship. Breathing also relaxes the body, which will help both people feel safer to proceed.

Once this awareness has been awakened, all the other skills of positive self talk make sense. I call them the *"Politics of I-Matter"* because when my relationship to myself changes, the way I relate to those around me changes, too. An old adage says,

I call them the "Politics of I-Matter" because when our relationship to ourselves changes, our relationship to those around us changes, too.

"We get from others only the degree of respect we have for ourselves."

When we reclaim our self respect—that is our willingness to listen and respond accurately to what we are really feeling and needing—then others are going to treat us differently, too. One participant was able to notice that sh*e* talked to *herself* with criticisms and demands. Once she heard what she was doing, she could by-pass the judgments and the shaming and just listen to what she was feeling and needing.

Welcoming our Imperfections

When we believe that we are good enough, lovable, and capable no matter what we have done, we are treating ourselves with respect (not denial), even when others may be condemning us for something that was upsetting to them. Welcoming our imperfection—when we forget, misunderstand, or fumble—can be an act of accountability for how our behavior has affected others, rather than a cause for inner shaming. We do want to let the other person know that we are aware of what we have done that has caused them trouble. We may even want to offer an apology. We can do this graciously, giving respect and accountability, without condemning ourselves for what happened. Who among us has not said or done something inappropriate at some time? It's OK, and so is making amends.

Having a safe internal environment is up to us. It is not a function of how others are treating us.

> *"Sandra, why didn't you call me when you said you would? I stayed by the phone all morning instead of doing errands I needed to do. What happened?"*
>
> *"Oh boy, I really goofed. I can see you are really upset. I just got going on this project and there wasn't a phone to call you and let you know my timing had changed. I needed to get that project completed then. I'm sorry you were inconvenienced."*
>
> *"Did you even think about me?"*
>
> *"Yes, I knew you were planning on the call. I guess I just made an assumption that we could do it another time. I can see now that my assumption had consequences for you as well as our relationship. You are feeling hurt and mad."*
>
> *"Well, I may not trust you the next time you tell me you will call me at a certain time."*
>
> *"You're feeling reluctant to trust our connection right now, and I will really try to be more mindful, and make more of an effort to call you if I need to change our plans."*

When we support ourselves in this way, we are not dependent on others' experience of us for validation. Then it is OK if others are upset by something we did. That is cause for paying attention to the relationship, but not questioning our self-esteem. If we can't welcome our imperfections, we are vulnerable to the shaming that will come when others are hurt by our actions. Having a safe internal environment is up to us. It is not a function of how others are treating us! As one participant put it,

"I have a gentler, kinder acceptance of my humanness."

From this place of self-acceptance, we can weather the storms of others' shaming or defensive behaviors, and communicate honestly and directly what we see, feel, know and want. We can bring our behavior to choice, while observing, empathizing and responding to what others are saying and doing. (*See chart on Honest and Direct Communication at the end of this chapter.*)

Belly Consciousness

Our body is our first communicator. It is communicating all the time! The problem is that we haven't been listening. Before we can give support to others who may be upset, we have to first listen to ourselves. This knowing how we feel may be easy for people who are in touch with their feelings, have words to describe them, and are comfortable letting others know how they feel. But in our culture feelings have been:

- Shamed—"Don't feel that way."

- Denied— "Really, I'm OK."

- Attacked —"Shut up!"

Boys have been told never to be scared, girls never to be angry. It became dangerous as young people to even know what we were feeling, let alone tell anyone. We learned to discount how we felt in order to be safe. Most likely no one asked us how we were feeling when we were growing up, and they didn't tell us how they were feeling. So we don't have a speaking vocabulary for our feelings, and the inner pathway to knowing them may be hard to find. This training tells us we have to know what we are feeling before we can know what to do. Hmm. How do we proceed from here? Carefully….

In the 1950s, Carl Rogers was making a radical shift in the field of psychotherapy. Before Rogers, therapists followed Freud's model of analyzing clients, diagnosing them, and "helping" them see what was wrong. Rogers believed the owner of the problem was the best solver of that problem, and the job of the therapist was to be a compassionate witness. If the therapist could understand what the client was *feeling*, the client would feel understood and safe enough to keep seeking the solution to their problem. Rogers saw the task of the therapist as creating a safe environment where the client could solve their own problem. The American Humanistic Psychology Association grew out of Roger's work and his leadership in taking the power and centrality of empathy out into the international community.

We want to match sensations with words that describe feelings.

Thomas Gordon, a student of Rogers, developed this approach in his training called Parent Effectiveness Training (PET), as did Marshall Rosenberg in his model of Nonviolent Communication (NVC). Taking the PET training was my most formative experience as a young parent with three boys under age four. It taught me that feelings are the basis of all communication. It gave me a sense of competency to handle whatever trouble was arising; a sense of how to balance my needs with my children's needs without reverting to power struggles. It taught me to hold relationship at the center of my communication and to trust that the one with a problem could solve it themselves with the right support. At the center of this awareness is belly consciousness—following our feelings.

Feelings Are Our Compass for Communicating

Whether we feel positive, neutral, or negative about what is happening is going to indicate what skills we will use in responding to another's behavior. Emotional literacy—knowing what I am feeling and what the other is feeling—becomes essential to our new way of communicating. A list of feeling words (*see list at end of the chapter*) helps us get started. But even before we can use the list, we have to be able to have this conversation with ourselves:

> *"Hello, anybody in there? What are you feeling? Hmm...just a bunch of sensations: heart beating, throat dry, palms sweating, head aching... feels uncomfortable. This must mean I'm feeling upset by what is happening."*

We have to go back to kindergarten, start slowly, and be willing to be a learner. We want to match sensations with words that describe feelings. We don't have to be right. We can guess.

Start with the four feelings that psychologists have identified as the most basic: **mad, sad, glad, and scared.** All other feelings are a variation on those. Count them—just four. Breathe. It's not going to be too hard. Think about what your body is doing when you are feeling each of those feelings separately. Now make a list of the ten feeling words you use most frequently. (My ten are: confused, concerned, upset, frustrated, annoyed, overwhelmed, sad, surprised, impatient, and curious.) That's probably enough. Don't worry about getting just the right one. It's not the naming of the feeling that is so hard, it's *getting used to the vulnerability of sharing feelings* that will be the biggest challenge (and sometimes will make your mind go blank).

Once we have our compass and we are able to recognize and name feelings, we can begin to construct a roadmap for how to respond when trouble happens.

The Principles and Skills in the CCI Toolbox: A Roadmap
(See The Conscious Communication flow chart page at end of this chapter.)

1. All communication originates with a feeling. We have to ask ourselves, "What am I feeling?" before we can communicate *accurately* with another. We will learn how to take responsibility for what we are feeling (not blame others), and support our self-esteem when we feel attacked so we can stay in an interaction. Our first skill is **positive self talk.**

2. How we are feeling determines what skill we will use. If we feel supportive and separate from what another person is upset about, we will respond with the skill of **Active Listening.** If we are feeling upset and need something to change, we will use a skill that initiates our request for change. This is called **an I-Message.** We will focus on this skill in Chapter Three.

3. Our feelings may change. We may begin an interaction by feeling receptive, but as the other person says more, we realize we are getting upset by what they are saying. When a partner complains that she had a hard day, we feel sympathetic. But then she complains that we left the gas tank on empty and it added to the stress of her day, and now we feel defensive. Being aware of these changes within ourselves is being conscious of a process as it unfolds. We are both participating and observing what is happening at the same time. This dual attention allows us to change from one skill to another as the situation or as feelings change.

4. If we initiate conflict we want to have a strategy for what to do next. We will avoid reacting to any defensive attacks, demands or solutions. We will listen for the other's needs and feelings—and reflect them back— so s/he feels understood and safe to stay in the conflict. If we focus only on our own needs, we may alienate the other person and end up in the old power struggle over who gets the last word. If we acknowledge their needs too, we can engage them in cooperating to find a solution that will meet the most needs and be supported by both parties.

> *It's not the naming of the feeling that is so hard, it's getting used to the vulnerability of sharing them that will be the biggest challenge.*

> *Most arguments are about a favorite solution which obliterates the other's needs.*

We call this skill **"The Dance."** We will focus on this skill in Chapter Three.

5.   There are two kinds of conflicts: basic human needs (not debatable) and values (opinion-based, debatable). A conflict of needs has obvious consequences; if you left the car on empty, it can't be driven to work without first stopping for gas. A conflict of values has less obvious, debatable consequences; *"You shouldn't say that, it's rude."* The other says, *"No it's not!"* Being clear about what kind of conflict is present informs what skills we use to address it.

6.   The key to conflict resolution is defining a problem in terms of needs rather than solutions. Most arguments are about a favorite solution which obliterate the other's needs. It is a skill to reframe problems in such a way that we can address it cooperatively instead of competitively. For instance, when one partner needs the car to go to a meeting and the other demands the car for a more "important event," they have a win/lose dynamic. Focused on the car as the solution, each will try to discredit the other's need in order to defend their own. When reframed, what they both <u>need</u> is transportation. When they can cooperate in considering alternatives, many become available and they can find one that meets both people's needs. They are sharing power in deciding what happens with the car, while holding both people's needs as important. This builds trust and safety in the relationship, and conflict becomes less threatening. The skill we use to reach this goal is **Negotiation.** We will focus on this skill in Chapter Five.

Holding both people's needs as important builds trust and safety in relationships, and conflict becomes less threatening.

7.   When conflicts don't resolve, we need skills to manage our differences for the sake of the relationship. These skills are about honoring differences, separateness, and the good parenting of our own inner child who may feel demanding or resentful at her needs not being met by the other. We call them **"Skills Plus"** because they are used to create understanding of the life experiences that are generating the values involved as a preliminary step to any possible resolution. In most cases these differences do not resolve, and the skill we learn is how to hold the differences without harming the relationship. We will focus on this skill in Chapter Six.

8.   When the consequences to us are too great to share power in deciding what happens, we are tempted to throw our skills to the wind and grab power to be sure we control what happens. We can instead be aware of the consequences to the relationship of that choice, and make it consciously. We use **The Non-Negotiable Stand Skill** to protect our needs in a way that minimizes the negative effect on the relationship of not sharing power in deciding what happens. We will focus on this skill in Chapter Eight.

With these skills, our communication can become *a work of art*. We will have choices about how to share power in relationships and how to stay emotionally connected in the midst of conflict. We can use conflict to improve relationships, deepen understanding, and increase our own self-esteem, while meeting the most needs of those involved. With this new way of communicating, we can create a more respectful and expressive culture for future generations.

Reading the Roadmap

We can use conflict to improve relationships, deepen understanding, and increase our own self-esteem, while meeting the most needs.

A change may occur as we are communicating. We start out an interaction with someone who is upset being patient and available, but as time goes on our attention shifts and we now need something else to be happening (like making a phone call we just remembered we have to make). Or it may be a change in the environment. The kids' table manners are acceptable and there is no problem until Grandma comes for dinner. Now the same behavior that was okay before is no longer acceptable. The map continues to guide us, no matter what the circumstances, with the simple question:

"Do I feel okay or upset with what is going on?"

When we feel okay, we want to be supportive and use the Active Listening Skill. When we feel upset, we want to use our confrontation skill, the I-Message.

Once we bring the other person into the situation with our I-Message, we are going to have double trouble because now we have to be concerned with what *her* needs and feelings are, as well as our own. How are we going to avoid the potential for an argument or power struggle? Breathe… right here is where the old culture and the new collide. We have asked for change and we have met resistance because there is a conflict of needs or values (later we will distinguish between how these are handled). Do we:

- Grab power to get what we want and sacrifice relationship with that person?

    "I said I didn't want to talk about it!" (Externalizer)

- Make our needs disappear to "keep the peace?"

    "Okay, I'm sorry I brought it up. Forget it." (Internalizer)

- Go into the positive self talk?

    "This is just a little trouble, and I know what to do. I care about both of us."

- Center ourselves for the work ahead?

- Confidently proceed with the negotiation skill that begins by naming both people's needs and feelings (sharing power in deciding what happens)

If we choose the latter three, the map guides us with the **Negotiation Skill** through the maze of conflicting needs and feelings to a new place where we can both feel okay about the outcome. If we pick one of the first two behaviors, we will find ourselves in the familiar power struggle of winner and loser. We will have another chance to practice welcoming our imperfections and refocusing on the map that takes us from unconscious to conscious communication.

We Feel Separate and Supportive: Active Listening

> *We want them to be able to consider how they want to solve their problem without any interference.*

The Conscious Communication roadmap shows us when to use which skill depending on how we are feeling about what is happening. We are going to start out where someone else is upset. We have checked out our own reactions to what is happening, and we feel separate, accepting of his or her feelings (not necessarily of the situation), ready and willing to listen. We believe that the one who is upset is the best solver of their problem, and that our job is to be a compassionate witness and to create a safe environment. We want them to be able to consider how they want to solve their problem without any interference.

We have checked our favorite barriers at the door (*"Oops, there's one that snuck in. I started asking questions. Sandra said that would happen; but I heard myself do it and I got right back on the track of listening for feelings again."*) We are not attached to the outcome; we are in service and need no particular results ourselves. We know that our good advice is not useful unless specifically asked for (even if it is good.)

Active Listening is simple, but not easy. Our goal is to listen for the feelings *underneath* statements of content, and feed the feelings back to the person with the problem. We want the speaker to have the experience of having a game of catch with *himself*. Each time he tosses the ball in the air, he sees it from a different angle. What makes Active Listening hard is getting our own agendas (the habitual barriers) out of the way. We don't want him to end up in a game of catch with *us*.

The "Nod"

What if we are afraid to make a mistake? We can't be sure we will name the right feeling. Our friend says: *"I'm fed up with my job."* Is she mad? Hurt? Bored? We're just guessing. We couldn't do otherwise. We may be wrong. Tell your ego to relax. This isn't a test for perfectionists; it's just two human beings meeting at the edge of their subjective realities, attempting to build a bridge of understanding. Luckily, our bodies seem to be programmed with a spontaneous behavior when we feel understood. *Our head nods.* Have you ever noticed? It really is quite remarkable when we become aware of this built-in signal that will tell us our Active Listening has succeeded.

We are trying to complete a circuit, just like the switch brings light to the lamp.

We are trying to complete a circuit just like the switch brings light to the lamp *(see Active Listening diagram at end of this chapter)*. When the circuit is complete, the light goes on. When a person feels understood, they nod. We want to understand what the upset person is feeling, because their feelings are the basis of their communication. But they often will encode their feelings in statements that make it necessary to guess what they are feeling. For instance, a partner might say, *"I had the worst day I've ever had at the office."* If we ask a question (barrier): *"What happened?"* she may feel cared about, but not understood. There will be no nod. If we decode the feelings behind the statement, and respond with Active Listening: *"You sound frazzled!"* we are likely to get a nod. Bingo! The circuit is complete. She feels understood because her feelings were acknowledged.

How do we find the right feeling? We have to empathize—that is, be aware of our own feelings in the moment as a guide. We have to ask ourselves:

> *"How would I be feeling if I had just said what she said?"*

Go ahead and guess. I call it "going fishing." Throw your line in and see what happens. It's not up to you to be right, only to experiment. Let your ego go for a walk and focus on understanding the person in front of you. She wants you to get it right, and she will reach out a hand and pull you to the other side if you are off a little in your guessing. You may ask if she feels mad, and she will tell you, no, she feels bored—or vice-versa. Don't worry. You can't fail, because she won't let you! She wants to be accurately understood, so she will correct you if you are off target. I call this nod, the green light in communication. When we are Active Listening, getting that green light is our only goal. Later, when we are not separate from the problem, we will still watch for the nod to indicate that it is safe to bring up our own issues.

"But What If They Can't Solve Their Problems?"

What if your little girl had her feelings hurt on the playground?

> *"Sally wouldn't let me play in the jump rope game."*

All of your cultural training in how to be helpful is pressing to be heard. Your own anxiety, stimulated by identifying with your child and not wanting her to be hurt, is calling for attention. Everything in you is conspiring to solve the problem—except the part of you that has now had some training in the importance of listening! You are not the one who was excluded on the playground—*it is not your problem!*

> *"That must have hurt a lot. You felt left out."*

You are having your own experiment with truth here: will she really solve the problem herself, without you telling her what to do? Breathe. Be patient. Wait and see. Focus on doing your work.

> *"I was mad. I thought she was being really unfair. I decided I didn't want to play with her anyway."*

Eight-year-olds have eight-year-old type problems. We really are powerless to change what is happening on the playground, and the daughter is the best solver of the problem because it is hers. Her unique feelings, resources, perceptions and options are what she will pull together to decide her next move. Our job is to be the compassionate witness, to mirror her feelings back to her so she understands herself more fully. Helping someone feel understood creates a safe environment in which they will solve their own problem.

My son Nathan was flying with me on a small commuter airplane when he was six years old. He looked out the window silently for a long time and then said,

> *"Mommy, when is the wing going to fall off?"*

> *"Oh Nathan, the wing isn't...uh... are you afraid you won't get safely to the ground again?"*

> *Practitioners of these new skills (new values) have to be sensitive to the readiness of the recipients and whether or not they give their consent to this vulnerability.*

As we Active Listen children, we are giving them words to describe their feelings. We are showing them that feelings are important, and that we believe they can solve their own problems. This is an invaluable training for life.

Resistance and Respect

In the old paradigm, we have strong inhibitions about revealing, naming, and owning our feelings, especially when there is trouble. It may be seen as weakness. There is a vulnerability provoked that is unfamiliar. Sometimes we don't feel safe identifying our feelings because we don't know what others will do with them. There is the potential for humiliation, teasing, or shaming. People may feel "therapy-ized," as if we are doing something *to* them. This is not surprising, since the skills did originate in a therapeutic setting. Practitioners of these new skills (new values) have to be sensitive to the readiness of the recipient and whether or not they give their consent to this vulnerability. One participant likened it to "trespassing." She said she always wanted to be sure the other person was open to what she was doing, so she would ask them if it was okay to focus on their feelings.

Our job is to be the compassionate witness and to mirror her feelings back to her so she understands herself more fully.

What do we do when we begin to Active Listen and the other person tells us to stop?

> *"Don't talk to me in that psycho-babble."*

Everyone has their own comfort level with vulnerability, and naming feelings does make us feel vulnerable. Because the person with the problem is unfamiliar with the new paradigm, they may not feel comfortable letting us that close to their feelings. People often are uncomfortable being that close to their *own* feelings, or hearing their feelings articulated. Because feelings are directly related to what we are needing, it may be safer to talk about what they are needing rather than what they are feeling. Or we could ask:

> *"Are you feeling upset because you are needing...*
> *(more time, a turn, a fair solution?)"*

Naming needs is not as vulnerable as naming feelings alone. If there is an opening to explore the resistance, you can try one of these approaches to explain why you are naming feelings:

> *"I was hoping to understand more of what you are experiencing right now, but if it bothers you I'm glad to stop."*

> *"I am learning to listen in a new way that helps me understand you better, but I'm glad to stop if it makes you uncomfortable."*

Remember that when we Active Listen, we are acting out of a very different value base. We believe that feelings are the basis of all communication and that when they are understood, the person feels empowered to solve their own problem. This will seem strange and maybe even suspect to people accustomed to advice instead of understanding.

What About Giving Advice?

Sometimes participants say, *"But I want to know what the person listening to me thinks. I want her advice or suggestions."* That works fine when the person with the problem *asks* for the advice. Then they feel in charge of their own process. Likewise, if we ask them if we can make a suggestion, they can say yes or no. The danger is in us thinking we know best what they should do. We never have the truth about another person, even if the situation seems just like one we had. If we give advice, we need to give it the way we throw pennies into a wishing well, letting go without attachment to what happens next. It's a nice story we tell ourselves about what might help. Then we go back to listening and reflecting feelings, where the heart of the matter resides.

> *Sometimes the person will realize a feeling she didn't know she had until the listener mirrors it back.*

We will find that as feelings are aired, understood, and shared, they change. Sometimes the person will realize a feeling they didn't know they had until the listener mirrors it back. This can be a real "Aha!" experience that can unlock new thinking and new possibilities. It can change the way a problem feels. It can clarify a situation that was confusing. It can make manageable something that felt overwhelming.

> A. *"I was offered this job, but I just don't know if it's right for me. It might be too demanding."*
>
> B. *"You're feeling hesitant, reluctant to commit to so much pressure to produce."*
>
> A. *"Yeah...I really like the pay and the prestige, but I wonder if I'd have any energy left to enjoy the benefits. I'd be working a lot of overtime and weekends."*
>
> B. *"You're confused about whether your success would make you happy."*
>
> A. *"The more I think about it, the more I know it wouldn't. I hate to admit it and pass up this opportunity, but I just know I wouldn't be happy in the long run. Now I know I'm not going to take that job."*

The presence of a non-judgmental witness can lift the load of doubt or fear when it is shared. Can you see what would have happened if, instead of Active Listening, the listener had asked questions like *"How much is the pay?"* or *"Can you negotiate for limits on your overtime?"* It would keep the person focused on the *content* of the problem, which doesn't help them know what they want to do next. That knowing is in their *feelings*. When their feelings are reflected back, they become more aware of the truth of their experience, and that helps them to make a decision about what to do next.

What if the listener had given advice?

>   A: *"You should talk to some people who work there."*
>
>   B: *"I feel kind of funny stepping in where I don't belong and snooping around."*
>
>   A: *"Nonsense. People do it all the time. It makes sense to find out all you can before you decide."*
>
>   B: *"I'll see you later."*

People are likely to exit when unsolicited advice is given, because it is missing where they are in that moment. It is introducing ideas they are not yet ready to hear. They either feel alone and unseen, or feel pulled into an arena where they don't want to go. Giving advice is slipping into that cultural habit of thinking we know better than they do how to solve their problem. It may feel good to us, but not to the one with the problem.

Anger

Interesting feeling, this one. Many of us have been so hurt by anger that was shaming and controlling, that we have tuned it out and just stop hearing anything that is said in an angry tone of voice. Others try to manage it by never bringing up a touchy topic. Some have rooted it out of their personality so they can't tolerate it in anyone else. All of these protective behaviors may leave us unable to function when anger arises. When we encounter anger, we want to have good strategies and skills to support both ourselves and the angry person. Anger is a powerful emotion. It helps us feel strong when we are feeling threatened. But it is a secondary emotion; we feel anger *after* we feel a more vulnerable feeling. We want to refrain from becoming involved in the other person's interpretation of the situation, and help them go below their anger to their more vulnerable feelings. When we notice that the person we are active listening to is angry, we want to become curious about what they felt *before* they felt angry. It is helpful to understand that:

- Under anger is *fear*; and

- Under fear is *longing* for an important need to be met

Take the example of the mother who loses contact with her four-year-old daughter in a department store. She is frantic with fear until she finds her; then she feels anger at her for wandering away. As one who is Active Listening the mother, listen to the difference between:

> *"You are really angry with your daughter for wandering away."*   or
> *"You were really afraid she was lost."*

Which one would help that mother feel most understood? When people have learned all the skills in the toolbox of conscious communication, most agree that the listening skill is the hardest to master. It requires the greatest degree of inner work to both keep our own issues separate, and focus below the content of what the other is saying to reflect their feelings. It is work. It is a choice we will make only when we have come to believe that when someone is upset, truly listening to them is more helpful than giving advice. What do you think?

COMMON "FEELING" WORDS

SAD	MAD	SCARED	GLAD	NEUTRAL
ashamed	angry	afraid	blissful	concerned
bored	annoyed	anxious	calm	confused
depressed	disgusted	frightened	cheerful	curious
discouraged	distraught	confused	comfortable	uncertain
embarrassed	frustrated	insecure	confident	uneasy
guilty	irritated	nervous	encouraged	challenged
helpless	jealous	panicky	excited	shaky
hurt	disconcerted	shocked	fulfilled	ambivalent
lonely	resentful	tense	happy	disturbed
regretful	enraged	terrified	loving	divided
sickened	agitated		pleased	doubtful
Desperate	alarmed		proud	uncom-
Unhappy	appalled		adventurous	fortable

ACTIVE LISTENING

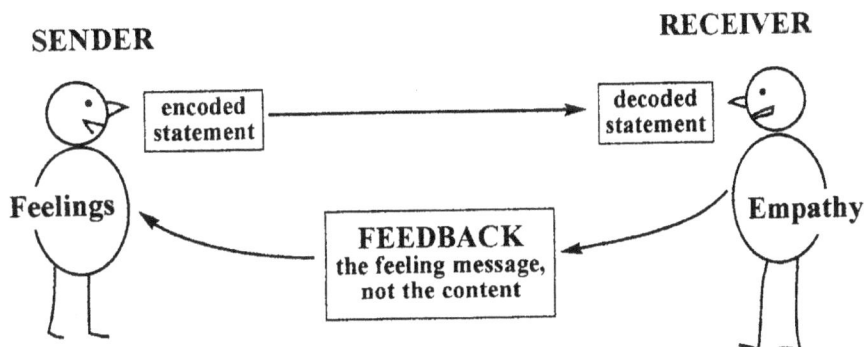

SENDER   **RECEIVER**

encoded statement → decoded statement

Feelings   Empathy

FEEDBACK
the feeling message,
not the content

WHEN THE CYCLE IS COMPLETE, THE SENDER FEELS UNDERSTOOD.

I have a
problem
with you.

OUCH!
I feel upset,
invested in
the outcome.

AWARENESS!
SELF-TALK
"Oh", Breathe,
I'm feeling …
because I'm
needing…

You have
a problem
with me.

STOP!
"Oh"
How am I
feeling?

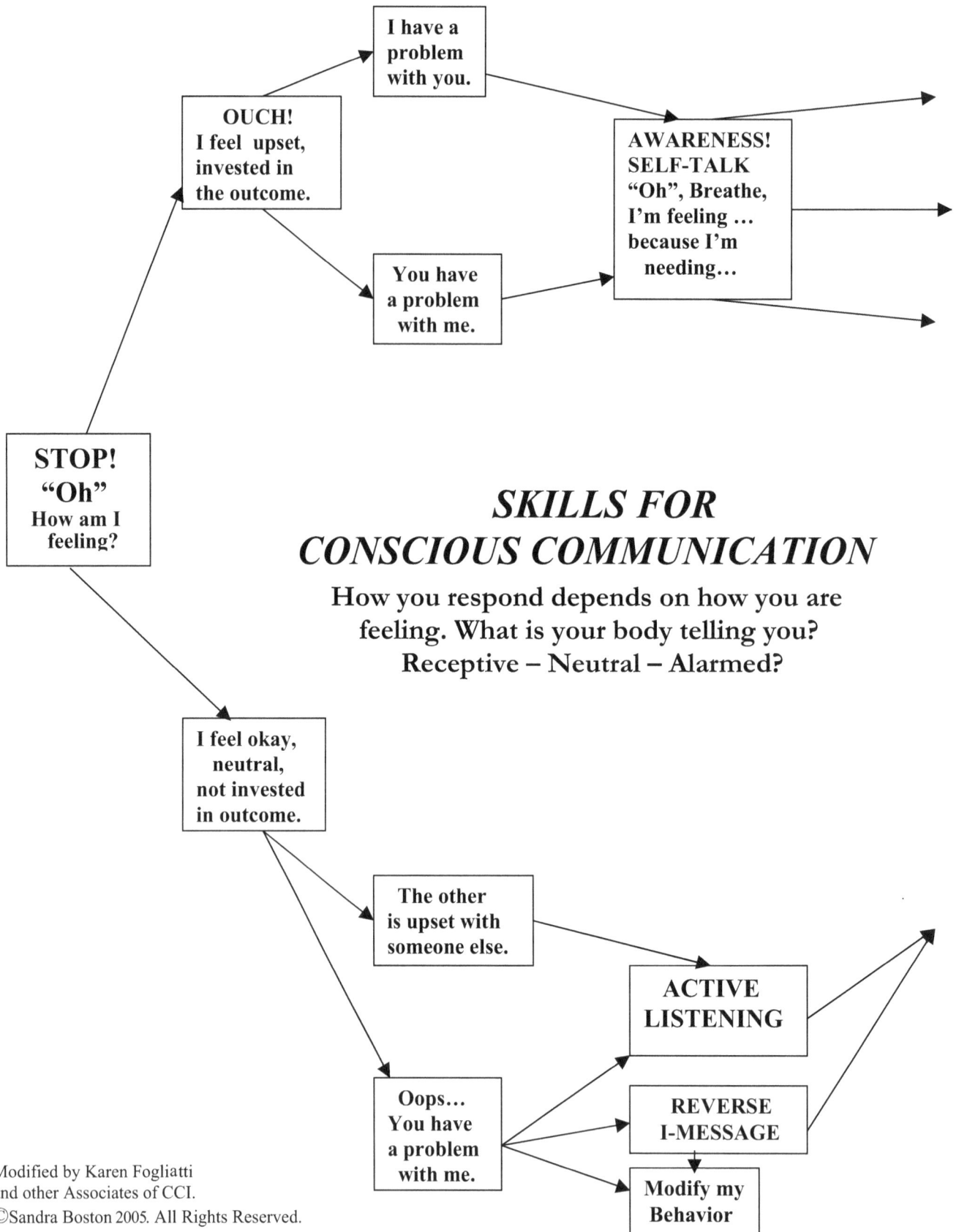

SKILLS FOR
CONSCIOUS COMMUNICATION

How you respond depends on how you are
feeling. What is your body telling you?
Receptive – Neutral – Alarmed?

I feel okay,
neutral,
not invested
in outcome.

The other
is upset with
someone else.

ACTIVE
LISTENING

Oops…
You have
a problem
with me.

REVERSE
I-MESSAGE

Modify my
Behavior

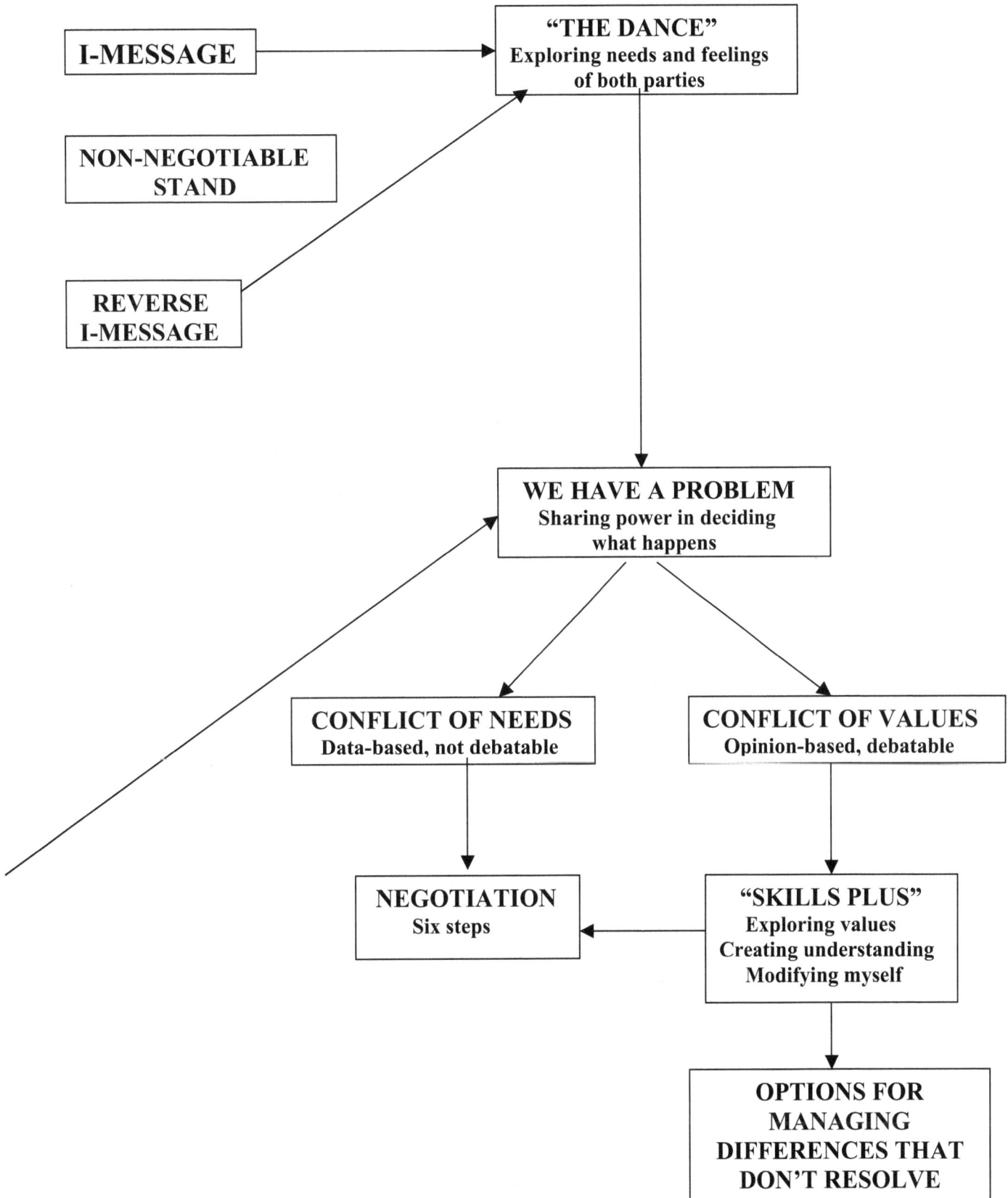

I-MESSAGE

NON-NEGOTIABLE
STAND

REVERSE
I-MESSAGE

"THE DANCE"
Exploring needs and feelings
of both parties

WE HAVE A PROBLEM
Sharing power in deciding
what happens

CONFLICT OF NEEDS
Data-based, not debatable

CONFLICT OF VALUES
Opinion-based, debatable

NEGOTIATION
Six steps

"SKILLS PLUS"
Exploring values
Creating understanding
Modifying myself

**OPTIONS FOR
MANAGING
DIFFERENCES THAT
DON'T RESOLVE**

PUTTING IT INTO ACTION - 2

1.   What is the basis of all communication?

2.   What is your analogy for being able to say "Oh" instead of reacting? It is like…

3.   How can you tell who is having a problem?

4.   What is helpful about the premise that the owner of a problem is the best solver of that problem?

5.   What conditions have to be present in you and the other person for Active Listening to be effective? What do you find challenging about allowing the other person to be separate and have their own problem?

6.   How would you begin to Active Listen if you feel unsure about what the person who is upset is feeling?

7. Is it ever appropriate to give advice to someone who is upset?

8. Why is anger a secondary feeling? Why is it more helpful to reflect the underlying feelings?

9. Write Active Listening responses to the following statements:

> "I'm so tired of listening to her excuses every day for why she can't get her job done."
>
> "I just can't go on vacation this year. There's so much pressure at work to make quota."
>
> "My rent just went up $400 a month. I'll have to move, but I don't know where."
>
> "I've looked everywhere for my purse. I think I'm losing my mind!"
>
> "I'm so angry at him for leaving me with this mess!"

THREE

STANDING OUR GROUND
WITH I-MESSAGES

We often avoid conflict as long as we can, because of our fear that bringing it up will make things worse. When we have a positive attitude toward conflict as healthy and necessary in any relationship, and we feel skillful in initiating it, relationships will feel safer and improve with the flow of information and energy.

"The door to change only opens from the inside." - Stephen Covey

"Conflict is the art of persuasion. If you want to be persuasive, you have to be open to being persuaded by the other person." - Gandhi

The Compass is Rockin'

We have learned how to recognize when we are not involved in a problem and how to stay separate in order to be most helpful. Now we turn our attention to those times when our belly rumbles, our blood pressure rises, and we realize that we are upset. *Our bodies tell us that now we are the ones with a problem.* We want something to change; we have an unmet need that is demanding attention. We want to stand our ground, without attacking or withdrawing. We want a skill that is going to help us take the "heat" of the differences, tolerate anxiety, and be able to think, while also feeling strong emotions. This is a big assignment if we are no longer going to pick up the weapons of the old culture: lies, threats, insults, abandonment, and rejection.

"I wish we could just learn to talk to each other!" This is a familiar lament when trouble arises. When things get hot, if either party defends by insisting on being right or by negating the other's experience, we have the usual situation of things getting worse. What we most need to learn is:

"Trouble" simply means differences of perception or expectations have arisen, and some important needs are not getting met.

Who will decide what happens next? In the old paradigm, the one with the most power forces their solution on the other and triggers all the resistance that the "victim" can muster. It may be a parent, employer, or teacher who is using the power inherent in their dominant role to get their needs met, no matter what the consequences to the other person involved.

> *Remembering at the point of conflict that we even have a choice beyond win or lose is a new consciousness.*

In our new paradigm, we want to share power in deciding what happens; therefore, we need a skill that supports us to stand our ground without taking ground from the other person. Given the deep currents of culture we have mentioned, remembering at the point of conflict that we even have a choice beyond win or lose is to access the consciousness upon which this course is founded. We are cultural workers, agents of change, and we don't expect our work to be easy. We know that every time we choose to be skillful instead of reacting, we draw closer to our high dream of a society where everyone's needs matter and everyone involved is included in solving the problem. The map for our journey is the Conscious Communication Model. The rudder is the question:

"How am I feeling?"

Point of Change: Gut Feelings

We are feeling our head getting hot and our blood pressure rising. Our fight or flight instinct is activated. It's getting harder to think straight. This is what it feels like to be the one who is upset because an important need is not being met. Now *we* have the trouble. Our usual cultural habit is to assume that, because we are upset, everyone else should automatically be willing to help us. For instance, my son is watching a football game on TV with the volume up high. I am mildly annoyed, but it doesn't seem worth the trouble of mentioning it. Then the phone, which is next to the door to the TV room, rings. I answer it, and suddenly realize I can't hear what is being said. My cultural habit would be to yell at my son, whose behavior I now perceive as rude and selfish. My perception justifies me being rude back. *"Turn that TV down!"* In that moment I am not aware of my body signals; or that not being able to hear is *my problem*, not his.

His response may be to:

- Turn it down. Hmm, no resistance. Guess it wasn't meeting an important need, or he is feeling shamed by my tone of voice and wants to avoid a conflict.

- Not turn it down because it's so loud he didn't even hear me. He needs more information.

- Not turn it down because it is very important to him to have it on that loud (Incredulous! How can that be? I would never need it on that loud!).

Here—right here—is the point of change: we are either going to use a typical, defensive block *("Didn't you hear me?"),* take a Non-Negotiable Stand (walk in and turn the TV down), or use a skillful way to let him know that *we now have an unmet need we would like his help to meet.* Which do you think would be more supportive of the relationship? In the heat of this moment, when our needs are not being met, do we *care* about the relationship?

In the heat of this moment, when our needs are not being met, do we care about the relationship?

"We Two Are One, Right Dear?" – Subjective Reality

One of my favorite teachers, Harville Hendrix, says in *Getting the Love You Want* that the hardest thing people in relationship ever have to learn is:

> **They are living with a stranger who does not dwell in their subjective reality comfortably.**

I want to expand this teaching to include everyone with whom we live or come into meaningful contact. Hendrix is talking about our unconscious assumption that, "We two are one, and that one is me." My subjective reality is the only reality there is for me. That is no problem, until I assume that my reality is the same as another's. When we discover that this is rarely the case, we feel shocked, even abandoned. We discover that we believe that:

> *"If the TV is too loud for my ears, it's too loud, period."*

> *"If I am upset about something, surely you are, too."*

> *"If your behavior is driving me crazy, you should know it and stop if you care about me."*

> *"If you love me, you should know what I want, so I don't even have to ask for it."*

Without a sense of separateness that honors each other's autonomy, we cannot stand our ground in conflict.

Sound familiar? There is no separateness, no autonomy of individuals here, and no boundaries that need to be respected. You are a function of me, and if you cross me, I'm entitled to tell you that you are wrong. Hendrix has another great alternative to attacking the other person's position. He teaches people to say:

> *"Given that you see it the way you do, how you feel makes sense."*

He is teaching people how to experience themselves as separate, and therefore able to think of the other person as different from them when conflict arises. Without a sense of separateness that honors each other's autonomy, we cannot stand our ground in conflict.

"Ouch! My Compass Is Gyrating!"

> *It is skillful to bring up conflict as a sensation in our body, and not as a condemnation of what the other is doing.*

"Ouch!" is what Arnold Mindell teaches people to say in his multi-cultural trainings when something is said that offends them and they want to quickly let another know they are upset. It states clearly, *"I'm here, too, and I don't see it that way. I matter, and that hurts!"* It is a quick, clean non-judgmental statement about ourselves. It is instant feedback to another that can start a dialogue about what to do next, signaling that we are upset and that how we feel matters. It doesn't say they have done anything wrong; just that we don't like what is happening. It is a skillful way to bring up conflict as a sensation in our body, and not a condemnation of what the other is doing.

"You are too fussy about how the house should look for my parents' visit."

"Ouch! I see it differently. I'd like a chance to talk about it and tell you why what I'm doing is important to me."

"Ouch" stops our natural tendency to defend by contradicting or creating barriers. Now the stage is set for exploration of what the needs and feelings are behind the attacking statement. Saying "Ouch" stops us from catching the ball, keeps us present to what is happening and helps us be able to choose what we will do next. We have chosen not to escalate the conflict.

From Control to Connection: Building Bridges

> *Our greatest influence comes in being able to just stand our ground, without taking ground from the other or giving up our ground in order to alleviate the heat of differences.*

In the new paradigm, we want to replace control with *influence.* Our greatest influence comes in being able to just stand our ground, without taking ground from the other or giving up our ground in order to alleviate the stress caused by the heat of the differences arising. Gandhi was a great example of the power of one person who simply stood his ground. He understood the process of change and the importance of vulnerability. He understood conflict as the *"art of persuasion,"* because he believed that everyone had a *piece* of the Truth. He knew that true change could never be coerced. Gandhi said,

"I don't want to win over the British; I want to win the British over."

He also said he did not care how long it took; he was more committed to relationship than to winning. Gandhi's only defense was his sense of the "truth force;" holding true to what he believed, but in "response-able" relationship with the British. There could be no communication without connection.

When a follower asked him what he meant by the truth, he replied, *"That which meets the most human needs.*" He believed the more force we use, the less influence we have. Never attacking the British, he always let them know what he was doing. He told his followers to act like free people in a free land—to do what made sense to them to meet their needs—and let the world decide what to do in response. His method was peaceful persuasion.

A generation later, Martin Luther King, Jr. faced the same challenges with his marches into racist communities. Someone said, *"Martin, you aren't going to change anyone's mind, and you're just going to get hurt."* His response was, *"They will know for the first time how racist they are."* King, like his mentor Gandhi, was using the power of vulnerability, and his willingness to stand his ground without threatening others. Many nonviolent organizations now base their work on the three "Rs": don't resist, don't retreat, and always respect the other.

In *Seven Habits of Highly Effective People,* Stephen Covey says,

"The door of change only opens from the inside."

If we truly want to respect relationship, we have to approach other people with the intention of persuading them to see things the way we do and to modify their behavior out of a consideration for our needs by their own *free will.* If we attack them, they are going to defend the very behavior we would like them to consider changing! Power and control may work in the short run, but they become self-defeating behaviors in the long run. When our intent is to build bridges and have influence, we can allow the process to take as long as it needs.

Not Attached to the Outcome

So we have powerful teachers—powerful not because of the rightness of their cause, but because of the strength to stand their ground for what they believed in, without attacking or avoiding their opponents. Gandhi said he didn't care how long the struggle for independence took. (It took ten years.) King said, *"I've already been to the mountain top"* the day before he was assassinated. Neither was attached to *when* victory would come. Each was committed to *a process*, and a personal discipline of nonviolence. Gandhi told his followers, *"Full participation is full victory."* That is the spirit we want to claim as we depart from our culture's messages about power and take on what is required to create responsible relationship.

> *If our intention is to share power in deciding what happens, we have to be open to being changed by the process. We have to be willing to "not know" how things will turn out.*

Our intention is to *share power in deciding what happens.* To do this, we have to be open to being changed by the process. We have to be willing to "not know" how things will turn out. We have to care more about relationship and respect for our differences than about satisfying our own interests at the expense of the relationship. A parent who took this course remarked:

"Hmm, I guess I have to decide if I want obedient children or responsible children. It's easy to get obedience –just use threat. If I want them to be responsible, I guess I have to be willing to be more responsive to their needs."

Attitude Is Everything: "I Respond, Although I Will Be Changed."

> *All the skills in the world won't help until there is a fundamental shift in attitude and in values toward the others involved when there is conflict.*

I was so moved by this quote above that I put it on my business card when I first began this work in 1973. It was written by a German-American theologian, Eugene Rosenstock-Huessy, who lived through Europe's two world wars. His statement sums up the essence of what we want to learn. Just being in our own truth is only half of the work of conscious communication. The other half is what happens when we enter into open communication with another—willing to listen, identify needs, and share power in deciding what will happen. In his statement, Rosenstock-Huessy is neither defending nor attacking. How can he tolerate the threat of losing? How can he be so willing to be changed in a culture that merits control and being right? He has departed from the norm and is marching to another drumbeat. He has abandoned the right/wrong power struggle and replaced it with an ethic of *response-able relationship*. His attitude toward conflict is one of *openness, curiosity, and vulnerability.* Like Gandhi, he is open to being persuaded.

Important teachers in every generation throughout human history have stressed that our *attitude* has the power to change everything. I imagine that this echoes from a time when there was mutual vulnerability and people needed each other for survival. I ponder how things got so out of balance, to the point where might and right became more important than relationship (see *Ishmael* by Daniel Quinn for a wonderful exploration of this question). Today, as a global community, we are becoming more aware of our mutual vulnerability, and many are now hungering for skills and strategies to maintain peaceful relationship in the midst of great differences. All the skills in the world won't help until there is a *fundamental shift in attitude* and in values toward the others involved when there is conflict.

In *Sitting in the Fire,* Arnold Mindell combines the principles of Taoism with multi-cultural conflict resolution. The Taoist teaching is simply to follow what is arising with awareness. Mindell equates "awareness" with conscious attention to creating understanding. He believes that people who hate each other (for good reason) don't want their conflict resolved. They want their experience *understood.* He believes that by creating situations where warring parties can be understood—their pain and rage empathized with—they will not kill each other. I asked him once what it is he trusts when he enters a room with three hundred people who hate each other. His answer was "mystery."

*The polarities
that arise in
relationships, as
in nature, are
natural, normal,
and predictable.
They are
opportunities to
learn, to love,
and to grow.*

Mindell was a quantum physicist before he was a Taoist and mediator. He studied chaos theory, and the deep, consistent patterns of the universal order (the Tao) that are present in the midst of chaos. When Taoists follow what is arising, they do it with an understanding that the same invisible patterns that order the universe are always present and can be discerned with sufficient awareness. Mindell says:

"The only purpose of conflict is to learn, to love, and to grow."

Even while we are intending to resolve conflict, we also want to accept that any resolution will be changed in the next moment by a new difference arising. He says nature creates polar opposites non-stop *in order to know itself.* In any "field," such as a relationship, a family, or an organization, over time polarities will arise. Mindell teaches us to welcome these polarities as natural, normal, and predictable, as opportunities not to control, but to learn, to love, and to grow.

This awareness is an extraordinary discipline to hold. How can these principles influence our willingness to *let go of the outcome*? More recently, Margaret Wheatley in *Leadership and the New Science* applies quantum physics theories to organizations and writes about the importance of systems being open to new information in order to grow and change with the times, and thus evolve. She states that a certain amount of chaos *needs to be tolerated* in order for an organization to learn and grow. Can this help us claim a positive regard for conflict? Can we see how essential openness is to our own growing and evolving?

"Have a Little Courage"

*Our compass will
relentlessly point
us toward our
heart, toward our
deepest longings,
needs and values,
if we follow it.*

A martial arts instructor who took this training suggests this phrase to her students when learning a new skill. Why would we put ourselves in the position of taking a risk that we might get hurt? Why do her students take to the floor knowing they are going to be tumbled around until they learn the new move? Look within yourself. Why would you take on stepping outside your culture, take on attitudes and behaviors that may be mocked or rejected? Why would Mindell call his book *Sitting in the Fire?*

*Ask yourself that question, and find the courage
that comes with the answer.*

You will need courage to tolerate the "heat" of your anxiety, and of the culture's resistance to change. In *Seven Habits of Highly Effective People,* Stephen Covey talks about balancing *consideration* and *courage,* the consideration to hear the other's truth and the courage to stand in your own truth. This balance is what we want to nurture, hone, and master as we take full responsibility for what happens next when we are feeling upset by an unmet need. We want to be well equipped to skillfully explore the differences. All of these teachers give us a rich heritage from which to draw conviction as we move forward. The word "courage" means "take heart" in French. Our compass will point us toward our heart, toward our deepest longings, needs and values, if we follow it. We must learn to aim our mind, with courage, to the heart of the matter before us.

"But I Didn't Mean to Say *That!* I Was…Hijacked."

We need something quick to say when there's trouble, because we are in a race against time with an amygdala hijack. Never heard of it? I hadn't either, until I attended a workshop on anger and was introduced to this term that explains so much of our behavior in conflict. The amygdala is the primitive, reptilian part of our brain that is programmed for survival, flight or fight. There is a nerve path in more highly evolved creatures that goes to the frontal cortex, where our abilities to discern, think, sort information, and make conscious choices are located. If we are sufficiently frightened (triggered), the electricity traveling on that nerve path is literally hijacked! You thought you were going to say one thing... but no.. now you are yelling—well, you are already lost in the amygdala! You are defending without ever having a chance to choose what you want to do.

The profound change we are reaching for involves changing reactions that are sometimes outside our conscious behavior and are rooted in our body's magnificent vigilance for our well-being.

This explanation helps us bring compassion to why it is so hard to make the changes we want in our communication. There is some humble humor in being able to come to class and admit you had a hijack last week. It happens to all of us. Together, we honor the profound change we are reaching for, which involves changing reactions that are sometimes outside our conscious behavior and are rooted in our body's magnificent vigilance for our well-being. We are hard-wired for the intent to protect.

Does Father Know Best?

Abraham Maslow teaches that all behavior is meeting a need. My son is meeting a need by having the TV on high volume. But we have all grown up in a culture where adults' needs are seen as more important than children's needs. There is even a word for this: *adultism*. It is like an agenda that every one knows about but never mentions. It does not honor the autonomy or the needs of dependent children. *Adultism* is unconscious communication. It is using the power of dominance to control an outcome to one's own advantage. Our culture gives us permission as parents to just bark orders. But, we don't want the end result which that behavior creates—children feeling oppressed, and their needs being disregarded. We want an alternative to making demands, threatening, shaming and trying to control the other's behavior when we are upset. We want to honor their separateness, their autonomy and to create influence and persuasion rather than control, because that is what creates respectful relationship. We want to make the leap to conscious communication.

"You Drive Me Crazy! My Triggers Are Your Fault."

> *Our triggers are the places of our wounding, where our self-esteem was hurt or our power shamed.*

Our culture has also taught us that others are responsible for our feelings: *"You drive me crazy! You make me sick!"* The implication is that if you weren't doing what you are doing, I wouldn't be feeling this way. Well, there is a piece of the truth there, that if you weren't doing what you are doing, I wouldn't be being triggered. But my triggers are about me, not about you. Can you make that leap to accountability? Have you noticed that sometimes what upsets you (loud TV) doesn't upset others? Have you noticed that some people have a great deal of patience with differences, and others are impatient with any difference? We will talk about the whole process of differentiation later, but for now, as we step into owning our feelings and problems, it is enough to just question how our feelings arise.

Our triggers are the places of our wounding, where our self-esteem was hurt or our power shamed. We may be afraid of criticism because our self-esteem was so damaged as a child that we no longer trust our own basic goodness and we live in fear of being discovered as inadequate. Any negative feedback we are given is going to trigger a huge reaction. The tip-off here is how big our reaction is. Sometimes we are just surprised or annoyed. We can still stand our ground. When we are triggered, we feel out of control. Our emotions are controlling our behavior. Our tendency when this happens is to "act out" our feelings, rather than focus within and compassionately notice how scared, hurt, sad, or mad we are.

> *Others are not responsible for our feelings, but equally importantly, we are not responsible for others' feelings.*

I find it useful to have a phrase that helps me go within when I need to. I use, *"Boy, am I feeling triggered right now."* It gives the other person information about me without any blame, and it keeps me focused so I can think about what to do next. It puts my attention squarely where it needs to be in order to stay accountable to myself and to the relationship. From there, I can move to more internal dialogue, such as:

> *"What am I feeling and needing?"*

> *"What do I want the other person to understand about me?"*

These questions help me avoid a shame attack and keep my self-worth out of the equation.

In *Undefended Love,* Psaris and Lyons have a wonderful analogy for a trigger. They call it a broken toe. They describe how one can walk around with a broken toe and it isn't much of a problem until someone steps on it. OUCH! Now, do we ask, "Why does my toe hurt so much?" or do we blame the other person for making it hurt? Whose fault is it that the toe hurts so much? Other people are just going about their business of meeting their needs. They are not responsible for the feelings that arise in us. When we are willing to take responsibility for our feelings, we become conscious of what we are doing and what we need.

This shift in accountability is a major change from our usual way of blaming the other. For some people, this shift is big. Not only does it mean that others are not responsible for our feelings, but also *that we are not responsible for others' feelings!* This place of autonomy allows us to respond with compassion to another's upset, without feeling guilty or defensive. We can allow feelings without trying to talk the other person out of what they are feeling in order to feel better ourselves. Now we are making room in our communication for feelings to be just what they are—information about how either our self or the other is experiencing what is happening, and not weapons of blame or shame. One participant put it this way:

> *"This is just a little trouble, and that's okay because*
> *I know what to do."*

> *Feelings are just information about how either myself or the other is experiencing what is happening, and not weapons of blame or shame.*

The Compass Is Pointing South: We Are Upset

We are upset. We want something to change without reverting to the old methods of dominance and control. We want to approach the other person involved in a way that will minimize their defenses and respect their boundary. We want them to be able to listen to our concern and have the freedom to respond rather than react. We need:

- The *awareness* that we are in trouble, and that it is our problem and not anyone else's

- The *intention* to shift our behavior out of the familiar cultural patterns and into conscious communication, bringing our behavior to choice

- The *skills* for what to do instead of deploying our inherited arsenal of defense

"Oh" Again – The Pause That Refreshes

In Chapter Two, we learned that this little word *"Oh"* is the linchpin for success in making the necessary shift in our consciousness from reacting to responding. When we are dealing with the other person being upset, the space after we say *"Oh"* allows us to choose to respond with Active Listening. We are okay, available, and detached from the outcome. This time, when we are the one who is upset, *"Oh"* may turn into *"Uh-oh"* or *"Oh my!"* One participant said, *"What about 'Oh my, my, my, my!"* Saying this seems like another way to breathe. It is shifting from reacting to being okay with not knowing yet what to do, and then slowly gaining the inner control to *choose* our response. We can take whatever time we need to make this important shift.

> **This shift to choice and accountability in our communication creates the possibility for a new, more respectful and empowering culture to emerge.**

Let's take the scenario of a friend failing to meet us at a time that we both had agreed upon.

- **Center yourself**: *"Oh. This is just a little trouble and I know what to do."*

- **Feel your feelings without acting on them**: *"I am angry because the person I was counting on did not come. Under my anger is my fear that I am not important to them, and that hurts. I'm really feeling scared that I don't matter."*

- **Allow your feeling to inform your way of communicating**: *"I want to use an I-message so I take responsibility for my feelings, and so I don't interpret the other person's behavior which will cause them to become defensive."*

Now we are exquisitely conscious. We are ready to communicate with an I-Message. We have a map to follow which guides us toward the outcome we desire—dialogue and mutual exploration of the problem:

The Four Part I-Message

1. When you... **"When we had date and you didn't come,**

2. I feel: *I felt sad and scared;*

3. Because I... *because I was looking forward to catching up with you. I didn't know what had happened to you, and I was afraid that maybe our date wasn't important to you.*

4. So what I would like is: *So, I'd like to know what happened."*

We are going to need the other's cooperation to solve our problem, so the more we understand about them, the farther ahead we are toward solving our problem.

A class participant who had been given a yellow card with the I-Message skill summarized on it, once referred to this moment as "yellow card weight-lifting." This map gives us several important directions. It:

- Gives us something to prevent us from using those familiar habits like:
  "Why didn't you call if you weren't coming?"

- Stops us from interpreting the other's behavior:
  "I guess I wasn't important enough for you to call."

- Gives the other person the information about us that will allow them to relate to us accurately.

When we initiate conflict with the I-Message, we leave room for the other person's experience to be different, room for them to respond without reacting, and to tell us how they see things and what they need. This is all valuable information for us in order to know what to do next. I liken it to a chess game. We have lots of options, but we don't know which one to use until we hear what the other person wants us to understand. We are going to need their cooperation to solve our problem, so the more we understand about them, the farther ahead we are toward solving our problem.

Our Map Shows Us How to Avoid "Making Things Worse"

When I took the PET course in 1972, Gordon taught the I-Message in three steps: what we see, what we feel, and what we interpret as consequences to us. He thought it best to leave the other person free to respond to our I-Message in whatever way s/he is moved to, out of consideration for our needs. In 1980, I studied with Marshall Rosenberg, who had added a fourth step to the skill. Rosenberg taught that making a request of the other person gives leadership to the conflict. It is not trying to control the outcome, but rather appealing to the other to respond accurately to what we are needing.

This request allows us to be more transparent. It gives the other person a clearer picture of what is going on for us when they can see where we would like the situation to go. It is essential that we make a *request* and not a *demand*. A demand is the old culture taking over again at the end of a vulnerable, persuasive statement. We are so used to hearing demands when there is conflict, however, that even when we train ourselves to make a request, the other may still hear it as a demand.

Because communication is about creating understanding, and what is said is not always what is heard, we need a process beyond the initial statement of our request. This is where I have added the fifth step of the I-Message: *Active Listening*. We have owned our problem with our I-

Message. The other person has heard us. Perhaps they will modify their behavior out of a consideration of our needs, but only if what they were doing was not meeting an important need. If we meet resistance, it is because they have an important need that they want us to understand about them, too.

> *"I didn't think we had a firm date. I was expecting you to call and confirm it and when I didn't hear from you, I assumed it was off."*

When we meet resistance, there is such a temptation to spiral right back to judgments like: *"This person is being unreasonable, stubborn, selfish...blah, blah, blah."* Not useful! I find it helpful at this point to tell myself that:

"Resistance is information."

It is information I need about the other person—her needs and feelings—in order to solve my problem. Any solution that she is going to support is going to have to include what she needs, too. So, I want to find out more about what she is needing. Active Listening to her response supports her to stand her ground and stay in the interaction with me long enough to name each of our needs and feelings.

> *"So you were expecting another call, and when you didn't get it, that must have been confusing."*
>
> *"Yes, it was. I missed a chance to go to the opera because I expected to hear from you."*
>
> *"So you missed something important, too."*
>
> *"Yes. I'd like us to be clearer next time about who is going to confirm our date."*
>
> *"I would too. Shall we make another date now, one we both know we can keep?"*
>
> *"Sure."*

"Time to Dance!"

After we have said our I-Message, we have to be ready to listen—with the intent to learn what the other person is saying. Our goal is to create sufficient understanding of what they are feeling that they will be willing to stay in this hot spot with us. I call this next step the "dance" because it reminds me of the Fox Trot. For those of you too young to remember ballroom

If we meet resistance, it is because they have an important need that they want us to understand about them, too.

> **The more we understand about our differences, the more accepting we can be of sharing power in deciding what happens.**

dancing, it starts with two people facing each other. As one partner steps forward, the other steps back. Then they both step to the side. Then they do the opposite. One asserts, the other listens, they step sideways; then the other asserts while their partner listens. It is graceful. It is effective. Both feel listened to; their needs and feelings matter. The Dance is where persuasion can happen. The more we understand about our differences, the more accepting we can be of sharing power in deciding what happens. This "dance" sets the stage for moving to our next skill, cooperating in creating change (coming up in Chapter Four).

"I Need More Information"

One of my first lessons as a parent beginning to use these skills was to discover how often I acted out of my own subjective reality. Because of these skills, I was able to shift into curiosity when I met resistance. The more this happened, the more I learned that, whenever I feel upset, the first thing I want to tell myself is:

> *"I need more information."*

> **My distress is generated by my perception of what the other person is doing, not the truth of the situation.**

My distress is generated by my *perception* of what the other person is doing, not the truth of the situation. One day I was running late and yelled up the stairs at my young boys to hurry up. When no one came down, a few minutes later I yelled again (not skillfully, still dwelling in my own reality with no accounting for theirs). A voice called, *"Kyle can't find his shoe and I'm helping him look for it."* My reality (that they were not minding me) was shattered. Now I saw their reality, and *my feelings changed completely. Whew!*

"It's Just a Little Anger. I Know What To Do."

When we are the ones with the unmet needs stirring up trouble in our bellies, and anger is our first emotion, we want to be skillful in working with ourselves. We don't want to use anger as a weapon to intimidate, but rather to work with the more vulnerable feelings beneath it. Marshall Rosenberg has a particularly compassionate way of describing anger. He says:

> *"Anger is a tragic expression of unmet needs."*

If we can use anger as a signal that we have important needs that we want addressed, and present them as *requests* for care and attention, we will be more effective in getting them met. Rosenberg also says, *"If there's anger in our heart, there's a should in our head."* Hmm. Think about that…when we are holding onto our anger, we are likely also holding on to our need to be right in that situation. *And being right isn't useful.* Anger is an important emotion, but holding on to it is not going to

> *Our anger is often our attempt to put the blame for our feelings onto someone else.*

help us to relate with empathy to the other person. We want to partner with them, not alienate them, in order to get our needs met (as well as theirs).

When the other person is angry *with us* we can say, *"Oh,"* then not catch the ball, let the raw energy of their anger go past us, and be curious about what that angry person wants us to understand. If she is angry with us, what interpretation is being made of our behavior? She is telling us about *her experience of us,* not the truth about us.

One participant realized:

> *"Just because someone is mad at me doesn't mean I've done anything wrong."*

She set herself free from the shaming that comes with someone's angry attack. How do we do this? After we do our positive self-talk to center in our own reality, the next important assignment is to look for the more vulnerable feelings underneath their anger. Kenneth Cloke says,

"Anger never rides alone."

The mother who has lost her child in the department store is frantic with fear, until she finds the child. Then she is angry that the child left her side. The anger is covering over her panic. It can be a relief to feel angry. Our anger is often our attempt to put the blame for our feelings onto someone else. Whose responsibility was it to keep the child at her side?

One participant challenged me about negating anger as an important emotion. He explained that in traditional Oriental medicine, where every season has an emotion, anger is the emotion of Spring. It is the shout of new life, of bursting forth, of energy released. It certainly is a powerful emotion, complete with blood pressure rising and muscles tensing. We don't want to suggest there is anything wrong with being angry, or that it is any less important because it follows other feelings. It is just more *useful* when we are seeking to understand the angry person to be able to identify the other feelings "riding" with it. I also find it useful when someone is angry to tell myself:

> **"They are giving me information about *themselves*—their needs, expectations, and feelings."**

Especially if they are angry with me, I have to remind myself that they don't know the truth about me, only their experience (interpretation) of me in that situation. So they are really telling me about them! A graduate once said:

*"Once I realized that conflict is not about my self-worth,
I could be in any conflict."*

That is a powerful statement. It is another way of saying that just because someone is targeting us, doesn't mean we have to agree to be a target. Eleanor Roosevelt once said:

"No one has the power to humiliate you without your consent."

Just because someone throws a ball at us doesn't mean we have to catch it. Are you still breathing? This is a pretty radical idea, and one that can keep our minds clear so we can get to the *"Oh"* of conscious communication.

I once attended a workshop where we were invited to take on the energy of someone with whom we had recently had a conflict. I chose someone who had hung up the phone on me. I was told to summarize her message to me in a phrase, to find a gesture to go with that phrase, and to act and sound it out with as much exaggeration as possible. When I had exhausted myself, the trainer asked me how that felt. I said I would never do such a thing. Then she said a masterful thing that I never forgot:

"If you can take the judgment off the behavior, and just experience it as raw energy, is there anything there that could assist you in your relationship with that person?"

> *Just because someone throws a ball at us doesn't mean we have to catch it.*

When the anger was seen as just raw energy, and not a weapon for a self-esteem attack on me, I was no longer afraid. In fact, I saw that I needed more of the energy of that level of engagement to stand my ground with that person. I was actually protecting myself by withdrawing from her, not wanting anything more to do with her. I saw in that moment that it was the judgment embedded in the anger that I was really reacting to, not her energy. This realization has helped me receive other people's anger in a less defensive way. When I can take the judgment of me out of it, it is not as intimidating.

Addressing the Quandaries in Conflict:

"I avoid conflict because it just makes things worse."

> *The I-Message helps us speak up for ourselves without fear of the other's retaliation.*

This is the untrained person's experience. They avoid conflict because they don't have a map. They don't know how to bring it up in a way that won't produce a negative reaction that *does* make things worse for them. When they avoid conflict, they also disregard their own real needs and feelings, making it even more likely that they will feel like a victim of other people's insensitivity. The I-Message is a skill that helps us speak up for ourselves without fear of the other's retaliation. Because our skill is to only talk about ourselves, and not attack or blame them, there is nothing for them to retaliate against. We are simply giving others the information about us that they need in order to solve problems. Assuming that they are in their own subjective reality, and it isn't their responsibility to be addressing our needs, it is up to us to build a bridge from our experience to theirs when we need something to change. Our map and compass show us how to address issues and resolve them, making things better.

"I can't talk to my boss like this."

What about a situation involving a workplace, where the person you are mad at may have more power than you, and complaining would be seen as out of order? This perception is often raised: *"I couldn't talk to my boss that way, he'd fire me."* Let's spend a while here. I think this is the voice of the old culture, assuming that bosses have more power and certainly don't care about our needs. Does the existence of a power hierarchy mean that I can't stand my ground with someone who holds a higher position? Will that be perceived as arrogant? Remember that we are practicing holding the other's best interest at heart when we initiate conflict. We are inviting that person into *an exploration of differences*, not a power struggle.

When we meet resistance, we are not going to react defensively, but with curiosity. Yes, it may be uncomfortable. The boss may not have experienced this kind of encounter. But you can be sure that you are not complaining when you are using an I-Message and offering leadership to resolve a problem.

People who raise conflict in organizations should be appreciated for their personal courage to stay connected to their own needs in the midst of roles and rules they are expected to honor.

I believe that people who raise conflict in organizations should be appreciated for their personal courage to stay connected to their own needs in the midst of roles and rules they are expected to honor. Our intention in raising issues is to open dialogue, to hear and respond to what the other party is also needing and feeling. We are not after force or control, but instead seek an improvement that will meet more needs. If we can have a positive regard for what we are about, I believe we can create an opening with the person we are hoping to persuade or learn from. I have talked to people employed by large corporations in personnel development and trouble-shooting. They teach I-Messages all the time to everyone they work with, including the bosses.

"How do I care about them when I am mad at them?"

Simply by trial and error, we learn that if we don't care about the needs of the other person, we aren't going to get very far with them toward changing the situation. Caring is an investment in the potential for a good outcome. It is a choice we make to maximize our effectiveness. When we have learned—and really integrated—that the other person is not responsible for our feelings, we are less inclined to spend energy in blaming them for what is happening. The Twelve Step program has a saying *"First time, shame on them; second time, shame on you."* Well, we intend to get past shaming anyone, but it is a good lesson about learning from our past experiences. If we don't like something, it is our responsibility to be proactive about changing it, not to assume that others should see it our way or care about what we need. So I may be mad, but putting blame on the other is not useful. Expressing what I need in a caring and respectful way creates the best possibility of having influence. Thank goodness for the I-Message. I can just begin with "When you..." without even having to know what I am going to say next. I can simply follow the model and fill in the blanks, knowing the process will take me where I want to go. I don't have to like someone to use this skill with her. It supports me in any situation.

"Conflict never solves anything."

> *Arguments are a waste of time, because now you know something more effective to do.*

Let's evaluate whether or not what we have learned so far has changed this very prevalent negative attitude toward conflict. My assumption is that people say this because they don't know how to bring up a conflict in a way that is going to respect both people and actually result in addressing issues and resolving tension. Does having a skill make you more confident to bring up issues? One graduate said,

> *"I am learning to listen to myself and my needs without fear."*

That seems like a million miles away from the person who avoids conflict. The antidote to fear is always action, stepping into unknown territory and having influence. Knowing how to do that in a way that will benefit both people makes the old power struggle seem so unnecessary. With these skills, you won't indulge in arguments anymore; they are a waste of time, because now you know something more effective to do.

The Versatile I-Message: Transforming Attacks

> *One of the most challenging moments for choosing to create peace instead of power struggle is when we are being attacked.*

One of the most challenging moments for choosing to create peace instead of power struggle is when we are being attacked. Something we are doing is giving another person a problem, and they aren't using an I-Message to tell us about themselves. They are likely to come at us with blame and shame, intending to push us to give up our ground. They may use angry voices, accusations, criticism, and judgments—all the cultural habits that block communication. They are making us the cause of their trouble. Ouch! Our impulse—our own cultural habit—will be to defend ourselves, to justify, to say in so many words *"I am not bad or wrong,"* because that is the interpretation of their attack we will most likely be making if we are on automatic pilot. One of my all-time favorite quotes from an advanced class graduate is:

> *"Last week my boss laid into me. I was scared, and I started to defend myself. Then I realized 'Oh, this is just an attack. I know what to do.'"*

How wonderful! There was a skill in her toolbox she could reach for after she was able to observe what was happening and name it. We have to know what the problem is before we know what skill we need in order to address it. One of the things I love most about this work is that there is a tool for every job. We are never stuck. This helps me feel prepared for whatever comes and I like that feeling.

An attack is just the other person trying to tell us how upset they are and what they need. They are telling us what is true for them, through the filter of their perceptions and needs. They may say it as if it were something true about us, but we don't have to hear it that way.

> **Our assignment is to not take their attack personally, but hear it as information about them, and specifically their unmet need.**

This takes some inner work on our part. The skill that is going to help us is called the Reverse I-Message, which was first developed by Marshall Rosenberg *(see Nonviolent Communication: A Language of Compassion)*. Just as we used the regular I-Message to support ourselves to stand our ground and give the other person important information about us, we are going to use that same skill to support this person to stand their ground as they give us important information about themselves. We will do it in a way that they can hear it without needing to become defensive. We are doing this in order to *maximize the possibility of really listening and understanding each other when we are sitting in the fire of our differences.*

The Reverse I-Message skill follows the same order as the I-Message, but it is safer to present it as a question, since the person you are talking to is mad at you:

> **"So when that happened** *(I did that),*
>
> **did you feel ...** *(mad)*
>
> **because you ...** *(were needing....or counting on me doing what we had planned,)*
>
> **and you'd like me to...** *(have followed through with that?")*

An attack is just the other person trying to tell us how upset they are and what they need.

"Oops...I Goofed"

There are two ways we can experience an attack. The first I call *"Oops."* It is when we have done something that has caused undesirable consequences to the other person and they are letting us know about it. We see what we have done, the consequences are obvious, and we are truly sorry. We feel understanding of their frustration. In this case, Active Listening is not enough to connect with their experience. It can seem trivializing, or as if we are hiding behind our empathizing and not showing up to meet them where they are. They want something more from us than just an acknowledgment of their feelings. They want to know that we understand the consequences of our actions, too:

> *"How could you have forgotten that meeting? We wasted so much time waiting for you, and then we weren't able to make the decision without you, so it was a total bust for us. We all have busy lives too, you know. I just can't count on you."*

> *"Boy, I sure am sorry about that. I can see that by my missing the meeting you were totally frustrated because you wasted a lot of time waiting for me and you couldn't make the final decision about the project. You'd like to have been able to complete that project at that meeting."*

Now we have laid the groundwork for that person feeling understood. Can you see the difference between that response and just saying *"You seem upset"?* The fullness of the response gives the other person the validation for their total experience, and it also brings the conversation around to a request. This gives leadership to the exchange.

> **Our self-esteem is our own responsibility.**

Now is the time for us to stand our ground; we are involved in the outcome, and we also want to be understood. Maybe we really did just forget and are embarrassed about it. This will be a time to welcome our imperfections, reassure ourselves that we are still good, caring and responsible people, and detach from the outcome of whether or not the other person can be persuaded to see us that way. Our self-esteem is our own responsibility.

Often we do have some reason why we did what we did, and we want a chance to give the other person that information about us. We will follow our Reverse I-Message with an I-Message to do this:

> *"When I forget an important meeting like that, I feel scared, because I've been so scattered in my thinking since that car accident, I'm afraid of what I will forget next. I hope you will cut me some slack while I recover from this thing."*

When they have more information about what is going on with us, they may see the situation differently and make a different interpretation of our behavior. We are creating understanding.

They still have to decide what to do about the project, but now the tension will be lessened, and perhaps trust can be rebuilt. Vulnerability—our willingness to take responsibility for the consequences we caused without defending our position—is what creates the possibility of persuading them to see us differently, and thus to restore and even improve the relationship.

"Ouch! I Didn't Deserve That"

The second kind of attack is when we feel unjustly accused, misunderstood, and *not accepting* of what we are hearing. Suppose we had worked overtime to meet an unexpected deadline. We forgot our partner had made plans with friends that night, and their reaction was an attack:

"You always just do what you want. You don't care about anyone else."

OUCH! That feels like an attack on our self-esteem. We think we are caring people who do not intend to ignore other people's needs and feelings. Perhaps there is something we overlooked here, but *what does this person want us to understand about them?* That question is our alternative to responding defensively with:

"What are you talking about? I do so. Didn't I do this and this and this your way? I can't ever please you!"

Ouch back! Now we have attacked *their* self-esteem. We have done what so many do in a fight. We have made the other person the problem. We told her that how she is seeing things is wrong. This way of attacking makes the classic argument. I call it ping-pong, back and forth: gnip-gnop-gnip-gnop. Both people are making the other wrong. It often sounds like: *"That's not true!"* or, *"That's not what happened!"*

Maybe we have to breathe and say, *"Oh,"* or was it *"Oh my, my, my?"* Maybe we even get caught in an argument before we realize what is happening. We can switch into the skills as soon as we become aware of what we are doing. Hopefully, our body sensations will tell us we have gone down the wrong road. Now we know what to do to throw that switch on the track and get into the station where that other person is hanging out waiting to be heard and understood. Here again, as with Active Listening, we have to empathize, that is, put ourselves in their shoes. *This means getting our own defensive agenda out of the way.* We can do this only when we have first checked in with ourselves, assured ourselves that our self-worth is not in the equation (even if the other

Nothing of value is created by arguing. Value is created by mutual understanding, and using that understanding to improve the relationship.

person has tried to put it there by attacking us) and accepted that we have to do some "work" here.

Why would we even *want* to get our agenda out of the way? That's hard work! We need a good reason to motivate us. *The reason is to protect the trust and quality of the relationship.* Arguing about who is right over something as subjective as "consideration of my needs" is a *waste of time and energy.* Nothing of value is created by arguing. What creates value is mutual understanding, and using that understanding to improve the relationship. That is our motivation.

We might just Active Listen if the person is only a little upset:

> *"So you are pretty upset by what happened."*

Reverse I-Messages are used when the person who is attacking is *very* upset and we need a fast way to diffuse the tension of our differences. When someone wants results, they won't appreciate just having us hear how they feel. Actually, when we are not separate from the problem, it is not appropriate to only Active Listen. We need to show up, and stand our ground too. But first we want to assure that the angry person feels fully understood. The Reverse I-Message says more than Active Listening. It lets the person know more of what we understand:

- **What happened:** *So when I worked overtime on Saturday*

- **How she felt**: *… were you upset*

- **How she interpreted it**: *…because it seemed to you like our plans weren't important to me*

- **What she would like from us**:*... and you wanted me to value our time together and keep our date with our friends?*

Acknowledging what her unmet need is does not mean we are necessarily going to meet it. It means we are *willing to create understanding and build relationship in the heat of a difference.* When we have met others in the truth of their experience, and we see the nod that indicates they feel understood, that is when we will move on to stand our ground with our own I-Message.

> *"When I see how upset you are, I am surprised and sad because I didn't know that staying a few extra hours was going to affect you so strongly. I'm sorry I didn't check in with you before I made that choice, and what I would like to do in the future, if I need to change our plans, is to call and check in with you and not assume it will just be okay."*

Now we are into the Dance, and, hopefully, because the other person is feeling understood, she will stay in the dance with us. As we dance, we are listening for the clues that tell us what the other person is needing and feeling.

Acknowledging what another's unmet need is does not mean we are necessarily going to meet it. It means we are willing to create understanding and build relationship in the heat of a difference.

> *"Well, I don't believe you. When have you ever put our*
> *relationship before your work?"*

Ah, breathe. One skill isn't sufficient here. Trust has been broken and it is going to take more patience, awareness, and skill to de-escalate the angry feelings. First, we have to not catch the ball of that attack on our worth as a partner. Then what will help is identifying the needs that are generating the feelings.

> *"So are you needing some reassurance that I really care about*
> *our relationship and will give it priority when we have made*
> *plans together?"*

> *"Yes, that's right."*

When she confirms that we are accurate, we are ready to put our own needs and feelings in the same sentence with hers, and we have then completed the first step of the negotiation skill.

> *"And my need is to be trusted that I do care about you and our*
> *relationship even when work is more demanding than I expected*
> *and I have a deadline to meet. What can we do to assure that*
> *both of our needs will be met when this happens?"*

> *"Well, I think if you just called me and re-negotiated with me I*
> *wouldn't be so upset. I know your work is important and I want*
> *to support you in that way, too. I just don't want to be left out.*
> *That's so triggering for me.*

> *"I understand, and I am much more aware of how important that*
> *call is now. You can count on me."*

> *"Thanks."*

Using the Reverse I-Message: The Seabrook Story

In 1977, I was part of the nonviolent army that occupied the site at the Seabrook nuclear power plant. Twenty-three hundred people were arrested that day in a very small town in New Hampshire. As I was walking toward the plant, a resident was out in his front yard yelling at us as we passed:

> *"Go home you hippies! Get a job!"*

I decided to stop and use a Reverse I-Message to make a connection with him in spite of his hostility:

> *"You're pretty angry about us being here. You're feeling*
> *invaded. This is your town and you don't want strangers telling*
> *you how to live your life. You want to be in control of what*
> *happens here. You'd like us to leave you alone."*

He kept nodding and answering, *"That's right,"* and after a few more angry comments, he looked right at me and said, *"Why are you people here, anyway?"* Ah. The opening that Covey talks about—the one that comes only from the inside—was there.

This is the moment when influence might be possible. This is the moment Gandhi hoped for, and King, and all those who trust that nonviolence creates possibilities for opening and for persuasion. I told him we were sorry for the inconvenience and that I understood how important the plant was to employment in their town. I was consciously respecting our differences, acknowledging that we each have a piece of the truth, and finding points of agreement wherever possible in order to build relationship *while* in conflict. We were then able to have a conversation in which he listened to my point of view about the danger of nuclear power and how it affects all of us, not just the people in his town. We parted as two human beings, holding our differences.

Fielding Hurt Feelings

Sometimes a person is upset with us, but they are not angry. They are hurt, confused, frustrated, or disappointed. This can be a big temptation to subtly use power by explaining to the other person why things are the way they are.

"I just don't feel like I matter to you anymore. You always have something more important to do than spend time with me."

"No, honey, that's not true. Yesterday was just a disaster. I ran a test and it failed, so I couldn't use the data to finish the report. I had to do it over again. I'm sorry. There was nothing I could do about it."

When we do this, we miss the person in front of us. We forget the importance of creating understanding before rushing forward to quell the anxiety created by the differences. I was once leading a training and in my anxiety about fitting the agenda into the limited time, I was rushing through some material. One of the participants had a meltdown. She couldn't keep up and she felt overwhelmed. She pleaded with me to slow down, and modify what I was doing.

"Please, Sandra, can we stop a minute. I just can't do this. I'm not prepared to do what you are asking. I'm feeling left out and like I'm a failure."

I remember becoming silent, focusing on my breathing. It was a hard place for me to be. I am very attached to completing things I set out to do. My Taurus nature wants to push through, no matter how hard something is. Here was a participant whose style could not meet me there.

In moments like this I find it necessary to give myself time to shift my awareness from my own agenda and feelings to those of another. Stopping my own forward motion when I am frustrated and trying to accomplish a goal is like trying to paddle against a strong current. After a few moments of silence, while I was doing the inner work with myself, I acknowledged her feelings, and my own.

> *"I see how upset you are. Obviously this isn't working. I need a minute to think because right now I can't see how to fit this in any other way. I'm frustrated, too. You need a pace that you can keep up with, and more information ahead of time about what you need to be prepared to do. I need to fit these assignments into a limited time. How shall we proceed?"*

But I didn't realize until later what a perfect opportunity it was to use the Reverse I-Message. She needed more than just her feelings acknowledged. She had taken a big risk to confront me, a very strong-willed leader with the power to decide what would happen. I wish I had said:

> *"When I try to go at this pace, it seems you feel overwhelmed because it's too much too fast, and you'd like me to slow down so you have a chance to really learn the material."*

As soon as empathy arises, everything softens. I was able to share this insight with her and the whole group a few hours later, and everyone felt a deeper sigh of relief. I realized that just by formulating that message, I had calmed myself, too. The fullness of the message helped me surrender less reluctantly to the need for change, and to even feel increased self-esteem for my new realization.

Enhancing Connection

Before we move on from the I-Message skill, there is still one more application of this very versatile skill that is important to mention. We can use it instead of praise when we are really delighted by what someone has done, especially when our experience is different from theirs. Remember when we identified praise as a possible block to creating understanding? It is only a block if the other person is upset. Maybe they think they did poorly on an art project, and we see that they are ignoring what was good about it and only focusing on the flaws. Our urge might be to point out what is good and try to get them to change their perception. This is missing what they are feeling in that moment, so there is no connection made. They will want to end the conversation with us because what we are saying is not helpful to them. If we use an I-Message, we open the door for another point of view, while not disconnecting from where they are:

> *"When I hear you talk about your drawing that way, I feel sad and surprised, because I see so many wonderful things in what you have done, and I'd like a chance to tell you about them."*

We have still left that person in charge of what happens next. We have not tried to talk them out of their feelings (hopefully we did Active Listen to their feelings before we sent our I-Message). But we have let them know that we see it differently, and we have made a request. That request is a powerful thing; it does structure the interaction, because it is what the listener is most likely to respond to next in the interaction. It is hard to dismiss a request.

We can also use a positive I-Message when we just want to tell someone how we feel about what they have done or what has happened. Instead of telling a child they were the hit of a show they were in (when we don't know how *they* experienced it), we can say:

> *"Wow, when I saw you deliver that line with such determination, I felt so happy because I know how hard you worked on that, and I'd like you to know how proud I am of your performance."*

That statement is just about us, and it leaves the child free to have a different experience. We are telling them our experience of their work. We are connecting our experience with their behavior, and leaving them free to respond in whatever way is authentic for them.

PUTTING IT INTO ACTION- 3

1.   How do we know when we are the one having a problem?

2.   What is most important to identify when we are approaching someone to initiate conflict with them?

3.   What things might I choose to say to myself before I start talking to the other person?

4.   How do we honor the other person's self-esteem when we are in conflict with them?

5.   How do we retain our personal power, even if we cannot control the outcome of an interaction?

6.   Why is interpreting the other person's behavior going to cause us trouble?

7.   What is an "I-Message opener", and why would we use this skill?

8.   What is ineffective about saying, "You make me sick!" or, "You drive me crazy!"?

9.   What is ineffective about saying, "I feel that you are being irresponsible."

10.   How would you respond to this statement with a Reverse I- Message:
      *"If you cared about me, you would have been here on time. I give up. I just
      can't count on you. When are you going to grow up?"*

THE GUEST HOUSE

by Rumi
in <u>Say I am You,</u>
Translated by John Moyne

This being human is a guest house.
Every morning a new arrival.

A joy, a depression, a meanness,
Some momentary awareness comes
as an unexpected visitor.

Welcome and entertain them all!
Even if they are a crowd of sorrows,
who violently sweep your house
empty of its furniture.

Still, treat each guest honorably.
He may be cleaning you out
for some new delight.

The dark thought, the shame, the malice,
meet them at the door laughing,
and invite them in.

Be grateful for whoever comes,
because each has been sent
as a guide from beyond.

FOUR

NAVIGATING DIFFERENCES:
"I See It Differently"

> *The other person is going to react to our I-Message. We learn to expect this and prepare ourselves to take the heat of the accompanying anxiety and tension. Because conflict is triggering, we learn to watch our own internal communication, maintain our intent to learn, and support ourself and the other to stand our ground.*

> *"I never realized how much the way I talk to others affects the way they treat me." – a participant*

> *"Once I realized my self-worth was not in the equation, I could be in any conflict." – K. Samuelson*

Because there are so many good teachers who have shown us how to handle conflict, it sometimes amazes me how little of their wisdom has been integrated into our culture. We still have so much to learn about the long-term effects of the misuse of power and control.

- We are fond of referring to the psychological birth of the ego as the "terrible twos."

- We predict that "adolescent rebellion" is normal, even though it alienates families and sometimes severs ties permanently.

- We settle for circling the globe with military bases (no other country does this) instead of learning how to live in peace.

- Alliances are made for mutual protection, yet our country walks out of them whenever they don't serve us because we prefer to build a better missile system, which is prohibited by international treaty.

> *We bring more awareness and compassion to the deep defensive patterning that is going to be our biggest obstacle to succeeding with the skills.*

A friend of mine commented to some German friends that "September 11th" changed the world. They said no, it didn't change radically for their countries, because they have lived with acts of terrorism, and they know about *mutual vulnerability*. They know that what goes around comes around. As a culture, we still need to learn that.

Put more simply, a parent in the training once said,

> *"Until I started using these skills with my six-year-old, I had no idea that how I talked to him could have so much influence on how he treats me. He is so much more cooperative when I take the time to listen to him."*

The mission of the Conscious Communication Institute (CCI) is to learn how to create peace in our relationships and communities. We want to create the safety, willingness, and cooperation to stay in a conflict long enough to create a solution both parties can support because it meets their needs and respects their feelings. This cooperation is where true personal and national security reside.

Differentiation: A Big Word for a Big Job

We have begun to practice the skills we need to stay in an interaction: the I-Message to stand our ground, and Active Listening to support the other person to stand their ground. We have a solid, affirming inner dialogue to contradict shame attacks. Now we want to bring more awareness and compassion to the deep defensive patterning and habits of reactivity that are going to be our biggest obstacle to succeeding with the skills. "Differentiation" means:

- I'm different from you, and I see things differently.

- I am a separate, independent person in relationship with another person.

- I am able to keep my focus on my own internal process, and act from my own experience of what is true, without giving my personal power away to another's way of seeing things.

Some people believe they can maintain their separateness only by cutting off contact; this is how they manage their fear of being controlled. They have not learned how to "take the heat" of differences and maintain a personal boundary so they can stay in an interaction and have influence. If we are not able to maintain our boundary, we will not be able to use the skills of conscious communication, because we will be too busy avoiding and defending in order to protect ourselves.

Boundaries: If You Can't Say "No," Your "Yes" Doesn't Mean Anything

There are good reasons why behaving autonomously within relationships is so hard. John Bradshaw, in *The Family: A Revolutionary Way to Self-Discovery,* explains how we all begin life totally dependent, and we learn by how we are treated, what level of separateness is acceptable in our family. We learn whether or not it is safe to disagree, or disobey. Long before the "terrible twos", we start saying *"No"* with our bodies. We shut our mouth to food we don't like. We cry when we are put down. We bat things off our tray when we are done with them. But it is when we start saying *"No"* out loud that we start finding out what it means to have our boundaries invaded. Starting to talk comes right along with this new and feisty sense of self. It feels good to say *"No."* It feels powerful! We try it out often. We are expressing ourself.

Families have rules about how much differentiation is okay, and they use sanctions for those who "go beyond the pale."

Right here is where a families' rules about differentiation are taught. Am I going to be able to decide when I am finished eating, or is there a right way to which I have to conform? Am I entitled to have a boundary? Does my *"No"* mean anything? Do I matter as a separate person? Families have rules about how much differentiation is okay, and they use sanctions for those who "go beyond the pale." Some families charge a very steep price for belonging. Their rules are rigid, and acceptable behavior is very limited. There will be a high degree of anxiety sparked by any differences. They will punish any member who doesn't conform. They use the threat of rejection and emotional abandonment to control behavior. This is the origin of the saying, *"If you can't say 'No,' your 'Yes' doesn't mean anything."* If you grew up in such a family, the very thought of initiating conflict will generate fear of rejection or being controlled. This legacy is a huge inhibitor to telling the truth.

At the other end of the spectrum are families that have no true boundaries; it doesn't mean anything to belong. No one cares who you are, what you are doing, or even where you are. This is psychologically the opposite of the first family. Anxiety will be created by the very act of belonging. A person who grew up like this is going to be afraid that relationship means being abandoned. Initiating conflict will be synonymous with heading for the door!

A healthy family has boundaries, rules and sanctions, but it also has a wide berth of acceptable behavior. It has permeable boundaries; members can leave for a while, try out new and different things, places, people, beliefs, values, and still come home again. In this family there is a low level of anxiety when differences occur. Differences are acceptable, normal, and open to discussion. People from these families have a high tolerance for differences and are more able to stand their ground when tension rises.

"Taking the Heat:" Tolerating Anxiety

So we are not all on a level playing field as we learn to stand our ground and take the heat of conflict, but we are all going to be challenged at a cellular level! Murray Bowen (*Differentiation of Self in Family of Origin*) and John Bradshaw both are teachers of how to free the authentic self from the bondage of the family system (not the family). Bowen stressed that leaving the system is not differentiation; it is just escape, and no patterns are changed. True differentiation involves *maintaining emotional contact* with family members while also staying true to our self, and *taking the heat of the resistance* of the system to our choices.

The process of differentiation requires the ability to:

- Tolerate anxiety when trouble arises; that is breathe, stay calm and able to choose what we do next.

- Take responsibility for our own well-being, and not have it depend on whether others agree with or approve of us.

- Take responsibility for our own triggers and not get caught being manipulated by another's behavior into doing things we later regret. We can't help having our triggers. They are the result of what our family system required of us in order to belong. What we can control is what we do with them. Anxiety will arise. Our habits of defense will activate in a nanosecond. *Whether we can take the heat of that moment long enough to bring our behavior to choice is what conscious communication is all about.*

How we manage our anxiety will determine whether we build a bridge or a wall in our relationships when differences arise.

Our ability to differentiate (or not) is going to *shape the course of our life*. It will determine with whom we can live, work, parent, share a spiritual path, learn from, or teach. Taking the heat is emotional work. It is being able to feel strong feelings (fear, shame, anger) and still stay in charge of ourself and our behavior. Our communication skills will support us, but the emotional work that has to happen simultaneously is what we want to bring awareness to now.

Our ability to differentiate (or not) is going to shape the course of our life.

"I See It Differently"

I was once at a workshop where we were working on healing our relationships with our parents. The question we were asked was, *"What is it you always wanted to hear from your mother and never did?"* As I thought about this, what came to mind were all the times my mother harshly judged my dreams, violating our separateness. When I told her I was going to go into the ministry she said, *"Where did you get all that religion?"* When I told her I was going to become a missionary, she said: *"You're throwing your life away."* What I wish I had heard was,

> **"That's interesting; tell me more about why you see it that way, because I see it differently."**

I wish she could have honored our separateness, seeing us as two people who had different ways of seeing the world, and bringing curiosity to our relationship. I might have been open to hearing her point of view, and even learning something from her, instead of having to shut her out in order to stay connected to my truth.

We can stay emotionally connected because we are taking the judgment out of the differences.

This phrase, *"I see it differently,"* has become the theme song of conscious communication. It allows us to stand our ground without threatening the other person's ground; it acknowledges our separateness, while allowing us to stay connected both to our truth and to the other person when differences arise. We don't need to get away to feel safe. We can stay emotionally connected because *we* are taking the judgment out of the differences. It de-escalates the tension that arises when differences threaten to move into right/wrong or win/lose dynamics. It represents a "both/and" way of holding two points of view—honoring the other person's right to their subjective reality. It creates differentiation in the relationship, and affirmation that:

> *"I am OK even if you disagree with me. You are OK, too. You don't have to change to please me or be in relationship with me."*

A participant put it this way:

> *"I understand now that my sense of 'right' and what someone else knows is right can be different without threatening the relationship."*

Marshall Rosenberg calls this "emotional liberation." The more we understand that our feelings arise from our *interpretation* of another's behavior and from our own needs arising to be met, the more we are free from either entangling alliances with or alienation from others.

What Drumbeat Are You Marching To?

It can be helpful to observe levels of differentiation in others as a road map of possibilities beyond our own experience in our family of origin. We all know people who seem happy most of the time, are able to roll with the punches of life, are not easily pushed off their course, and seem genuinely confident. This isn't because they have no stress in their life; it's because of how they handle stress. They have a high level of differentiation; they can take the heat of differences without being thrown off their own center—the truth of their own experience.

We also know people who are high-strung, irritable, upset by small glitches, and always anticipating the worst. They usually have very rigid ideas of how things *should* be, and can't tolerate things being otherwise. These people have few resources for tolerating differences. They feel buffeted about by life, and defensive about their own experience of what is true. There is a continuum between these two polarities, where we can all find ourselves.

We start out *inheriting our level of differentiation* from our families. We learn how to manage anxiety by imitating our primary caretakers. There is no reason to blame ourselves for our habitual response to criticism and judgment. But it is time to take responsibility, and realize that we can change the way we repeatedly respond to the stress of differences. I may be just as afraid to speak my truth now as I was when I was two, because of what I was taught then about the "right" way to be and to belong in my family. But I now know how to accept my habitual fear and not act on it. I have options. My *"No"* means something because I know I matter and I am no longer on automatic pilot. I am making my own rules about belonging.

> *Having a boundary means I say what I mean; I can take the heat of someone disagreeing with me without it sending me back into my two-year old self.*

Having a boundary means I say what I mean; I can take the heat of someone disagreeing with me without it sending me back into my two-year-old self. Boundaries are what make adult relationships work. Having the freedom to be true to ourselves and not be expected to conform to another's perceptions or feelings is essential to a healthy relationship. It's okay, too, if that other person really disagrees with me and would like me to change what I am doing, because I know what to do. I tell them: *"I see it differently."* I stand my ground. I am safe.

Welcome to your own level of differentiation. We are most comfortable with people who are just like we are. Who do you feel comfortable around? Who do you feel uncomfortable around? How do you compare your behavior to those two extremes? What behavior do you admire? To what behaviors do you feel aversion? As grown-ups, we are now free to choose our role models. With awareness, we can expand our humanity to hold more differences without reacting. The skills of conscious communication help us to replace our habits of avoidance with awareness and choice. This brings more intimacy, honesty, trust and a sense of security in our most important relationships.

 I have a friend whose response to most differences is, "I really don't mind." When I began noticing this, I commented to her about how often she said that and asked her if she really meant it. I thought she was just being accommodating, perhaps at her own expense. I wondered if she was letting me take advantage of her.

Over time, as I grew to know her more, I trusted that she really meant it. Then I began to appreciate what the Buddhists call "empty boat." This means you are free from internal demands for things to go a certain way, and you can allow the current to take you. You have no driving demands to paddle, to get somewhere other than where you are. My friend is like that. Being in her presence is like swinging in a hammock. She does not generate stress in relationships or in her environment. She teaches me about acceptance, grace, and yes—the power of differentiation to shape the course of our lives.

Teenagers Can Be Experts— So Get Ready!

In the study of human development, it is interesting to note that the teen-age differentiation process is seen as a recapitulation of the first experience of differentiation at two years old. A person is likely to act in the second stage in similar ways as they did in the first. Aha! That gives us parents, who maybe were not so smart the first time around, a chance to do the second round with more awareness and wisdom, holding differences without judging or punishing.

When my youngest son was sixteen, I was driving him to the airport to visit his father. He was ten minutes late leaving the house. I was already in the car, fuming about having to rush to be on time. When he saw that I was all heated up about it, he calmly said, *"Mom, are there any strong consequences to you if I miss the plane?"* Stopped in my tracks, I had to admit there were none (though *he* might have to wait in the airport for the next flight). He said, *"Then why are you so upset?"* He understood differentiation! I was upset because I thought his problem was my problem. He pointed out what I was doing, and the trouble was over. I was able to gracefully retreat, change the subject, and enjoy the ride to the airport after all.

I thought quietly to myself, *"Who is this talking?"* He was now modeling for me the skills I had taught him growing up. He had learned to think about what was going on instead of just reacting to another person's upset. He stood his ground, and stayed separate from me without becoming over-involved in my feelings.

Practicing the art of persuasion means being open to being persuaded myself.

Perhaps the most poignant experience of differentiation I ever had was when the Persian Gulf War loomed on the horizon in 1990. My family, with three sons, was gathering for Christmas. The boys were 20, 21, and 23. I was scared. They seemed oblivious to what was coming toward them. I called for a family council about how they were going to respond if the crisis demanded their participation. I am a long-time peace activist who participated in civil disobedience to protest the deployment of cruise missiles to Europe in 1983. I really worked hard to restrain my anger in order to bring any curiosity to this encounter. I was breathing very consciously, practicing every skill I knew about separateness, standing my ground, and practicing the *art* of persuasion, which meant being open to being persuaded myself.

We asked the boys to tell us what they would do if the draft was reinstated and they were called to serve. We knew we didn't have any control over their decision, but that we had a right to know how they were thinking about it, and we wanted a chance to have influence. One said he would go to war if he were called because it was the right thing to do. Another said not to worry, he would just go to Canada (oblivious that this was no longer an option), and the third said he didn't know. I offer this as an example of differentiation in a family—we sure had it! I Active Listened my eldest son, hearing his courage to live high ethical values. When I asked him what he thought about *why* he would be asked to make that sacrifice, his response was, *"That doesn't matter."* There was a lot of heat in that moment for me. Part of me wanted to scream, *"NO!"* But a wiser part brought awareness to our differences, as well as respect for his right to see things the way he did *as a member of our family.* In that moment, I understood, for the first time, that motherhood really is a give-away. His life is his, to do with as he sees fit. It is not a comfortable carbon copy of mine. I felt in every cell of my body how differentiation is emotional *work.* Acceptance is respect. Respect is love.

Curiosity Is a Gift

Didn't we grow up with the cultural stereotype that "curiosity killed the cat?" Isn't that a warning not to be too curious? How often do we notice that we have overlooked something we don't understand about what someone did or said? Could it be that that cultural message is running subliminally, especially if to be curious—to call attention to something that may illuminate a difference—might cause "just a little trouble?" Breathe…looks like we have some paradigm shifting to do if we really want to create authentic and transparent relationships.

> *We can't be genuinely curious until we have differentiated enough, and we are freed from our worst fear of not belonging.*

I think curiosity is the greatest gift we can give another person when there is conflict. It is an affirmation of relationship. It is the essence of the intent to learn. When Arnold Mindell says he trusts "mystery," he is being curious. When I am willing to fox trot with you, I am being curious about how we can move together. When I support you to stay in a conflict with me because I need your help to solve my problem, I am curious about what will work for both of us. Power and control—the old way—is devoid of curiosity. Any argument that vies for right and wrong is void of curiosity. Creativity thrives on curiosity. Relationship thrives on curiosity. I believe we can't be genuinely curious until we have differentiated enough, and we are freed from our worst fear of not belonging, which we learned in our family of origin. That is why it is important to take the time to focus on our personal experience, and bring compassion to why adopting these precious and powerful skills is sometimes so hard. It helps to identify what we have to *unlearn* before we can successfully integrate the new.

Meditation Is "Aiming the Mind"

> *The degree of wisdom we attain in our life is the degree to which we are able to discipline our mind.*

I believe the Buddha used this phrase in his teaching. How perfect it is for our purpose. I found myself wondering recently if the degree of wisdom we attain in our life is the degree to which we are able to discipline our mind. Meditation is the practice of disciplining the mind. Learning to observe our own minds expands our resources for living. It sharpens our awareness. It supports the experience of having choice. Learning to observe our thoughts without judging or acting to fix or change anything is a kind of freedom from impulse. In meditation, we experience the body as a messenger; it is teeming with sensations. But it is not our choosing will. As we learn to observe our mind, and thus know that we are more than our mind, we find the source of will that can help us bring our behavior to choice. Through meditation, we can contact soul, inner peace, and states of being that the ego cannot attain.

The practice of meditation may seem like a far cry from communication skills, but to me they are companions on the path. You can get to the same destination many ways, but why not travel on one with seasoned experience? Buddhism teaches that true peace is attained by being in equanimity with what is, making it neither good nor bad. It neither condemns nor denies anything. There is not a perfect way things should be. There is freedom from suffering in this way of being. It is a spiritual practice. When our mind is our ally, then anxiety cannot take us for a ride and dump us where we don't want to be. What part of us decides whether our mind is our ally or not? Who aims the mind? This is what the path of meditation teaches. I recommend that you investigate this practice.

AN AUTOBIOGRAPHY IN FIVE CHAPTERS

CHAPTER ONE

I walk down the street.
There is a deep hole in the sidewalk.
I fall in.
I am lost. I am helpless.
It isn't my fault.
It takes forever to find a way out.

CHAPTER TWO

I walk down the same street.
There is a deep hole in the sidewalk.
I pretend I don't see it.
I fall in, again.
I can't believe I am in this same place.
But it isn't my fault.
It still takes a long time to get out.

CHAPTER THREE

I walk down the same street.
There is a deep hole in the sidewalk.
I see it is there.
I fall in. It's a habit, but my eyes are open.
I know where I am.
It is my fault.
I get out immediately.

CHAPTER FOUR

I walk down the same street
There is a deep hole in the sidewalk.
I walk around it.

CHAPTER FIVE

I walk down a different street.

- Portia Nelson
A Hole in the Sidewalk

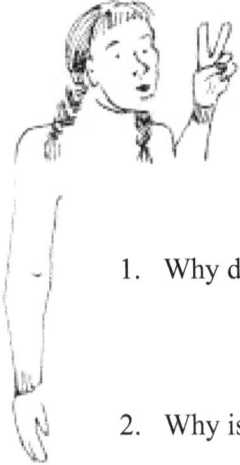

PUTTING IT INTO ACTION- 4

1. Why do we want to avoid using feeling words such as "abandoned, threatened, or thwarted?"

2. Why is interpreting another's behavior a drawback to good communication?

3. Why is a "You-Message" going to get you into trouble?

4. How would you define "Differentiation?"

5. How does your ability to differentiate affect your skill in handling conflict?

6. What beliefs do you have that might make holding healthy boundaries difficult?

7. What do you do when someone challenges your boundary?

COMMUNICATION

It makes your palms sweat,
your stomach tight.

It makes you sigh with relief.

It can alter the way you feel
and the way you act.

It's what creates relationships
and also what can destroy them.

It can make you do things you would never do.

It's something we succeed at one minute
and fail at the next.

It sorts out confusion, clarifies the mysterious
and has the power to resolve any breakdown.

It can build bridges
and tear down walls.

It's what gives life to our deepest aspirations
and our wildest dreams.

It has the power to create and to alter
the very nature of what is possible.

- Anonymous

FIVE

NEGOTIATION:

COOPERATING IN CREATING CHANGE

> *Since the whole process of conflict happens when someone needs change, resolution can only happen when others involved have been persuaded to cooperate with that change. The process of resolution involves acknowledging how that change will impact them, and what needs of theirs must be part of the process of change. If you have done that step well, and have created an ally instead of an opponent, the next step really is simple! (If not, go back to Go…)*

"All behavior is meeting a need." – Abraham Maslow

"In conflict, the greatest virtue is fluidity." – Arnold Mindell

As we move farther into our map of conscious communication, we are at a point where we have stood our ground, the other has responded (or reacted), and our goal is to share power in a way that creates win/win dynamics. We need to replace the typical power struggles and right/wrong thinking that create win/lose dynamics. This will require a consciousness about how power is being expressed by each person in the interaction.

Power = the ability to determine what happens

In the Culture of Control, members of dominant groups wield the power to make things go their way. Our first experiences of power struggles were with our parents, and we were often the losers. We adapted to this power imbalance with habits of fight, flight, or submission. Sometimes we accepted their dominance, too, because having the parents firmly in control made us feel secure. Sometimes their judgments made sense to us and we were persuaded to yield our position.

But when *important needs* of ours were overridden, we were left with unresolved feelings of disempowerment, which became lodged in our body as triggers of rage or grief. It is amazing what influence these early experiences of having our power taken away have on us as our life progresses! These triggers can go off under similar circumstances at any time in our adult lives, and we regress to a very young age in an instant. Just as we did in childhood, we find ourselves acting out of that same disempowerment by fighting, fleeing, or submitting. Our behavior is then very ineffective in supporting our needs as adults. We want to learn skills that will help us to never put other people, especially children, in that losing position in the first place. As parents, or those who have more power in any relationship, we want to be mindful of the power imbalance, and have skills to *empower* those we have differences with by recognizing and validating their needs along with our own.

I recently showed a video of these skills to a group where one person thought the idea of sharing power with children was ludicrous. He said, "That's not a parent's job." As he sees it, the parents' role is to know what is right for a child and make them do it. I observed my anxiety about his comment, the remnants of shaming still left in my body. I noted it with compassion, creating a safe internal environment for myself in the presence of his differences with my values and my life's work. I quietly chose not to catch the ball. If I had responded, I would have begun with,

> *"I'm curious about why you think that. Could you tell me more about why you think parents always know what is right for their kids, because I see it differently?"*

Then I would have Active Listened to the feelings within his response. This was a conversation where nothing needed to be decided, so it would have been just an exploration of our differences. If we were parenting together, we might have to negotiate how we were going to handle our child not eating his dinner, or not wanting to go to bed when we thought was best.

I was reminded of the father in one of my classes who said:

> *"I guess I have to decide if I want obedient children or responsible children."*

If we share power in deciding what happens, then both people's needs are going to be important and will be included in the solution. The other person will want to stay in the process with us. She will feel respected and important, and that her needs matter. This builds life-long trust, and loving relationships. Without this, we are left with winners and losers and people get out of those relationships as soon as they can.

The Negotiation Skill: Creating Cooperation

Often, when we hit a hot spot with someone we know and trust, we are able to float a solution that works for both people. The trouble is adjusted, and we move on. Would that this were always the case! More often, trust is shaken when a difference arises, and we are going to need skills to navigate the course through the trouble. This will be especially true in a relationship where there is low trust to begin with. The good news is that we have already acquired the skills that we will need to create cooperation instead of power struggle. What we will learn now is a progression to follow in reaching our goal, which is a solution that addresses the needs of both parties. There are six steps to follow:

(These steps are adapted from Thomas Gordon's Problem Ownership Model described in *Parent Effectiveness Training.* See bibliography.)

1. **Identifying** the unmet needs of each person and putting them side by side in importance (eliminating rank as a solution.)

2. **Exploring** possible solutions without evaluating

3. **Evaluating** by eliminating any suggestions that either party cannot agree to

4. **Choosing** a mutually agreeable solution or combination from those remaining

5. **Implementing**: who will do what by when

6. **Contracting** for a time to check back and see if the problem is solved or if it needs to be re-negotiated based on new information or a change of needs.

We will most often find ourselves well into an argument before we realize that we need to use some skills. These steps give us the map for how to put the brakes on and shift from our predictable focus on solutions to an awareness of the needs that are motivating them.

A solution is an action taken to meet a need. When our solution doesn't work for the other person, because it is threatening a need of theirs, what we really have is a conflict of needs.

Step One: From Struggle to Skill, From Solutions to Needs

I used to struggle to get my kids to bed by 7:30, so I would have some evening time before I fell into bed exhausted. It was a grand power struggle over who would decide what happens, from me yelling threats, to one of them fighting with the other, to one more drink of water, yada, yada, yada. We were arguing about solutions: "Go to bed" and "I don't want to." It was a win/lose situation where they only capitulated after they exhausted every option imaginable. And there were three of them!

Solutions are what we decide to do to meet our needs. Unfortunately, we don't know that until we get training in how to listen for the needs beneath the solutions. Arguments are always about solutions; conflicts are always about unmet needs. If we can learn how to guide the argument into an exploration of needs, we can begin to create cooperation in solving the problem. Why? Because when people experience their needs being addressed, they are more willing to give their attention and cooperation to the process.

A solution is an action to meet a need. It is what we do after we feel a need. If we close our eyes and check in with our body awareness, most often we will find that solutions arise in our heads, in our thought process. Needs are very different. They are a sensing that something we perceive as necessary is missing. They first arise as a feeling, an upset in the homeostasis of our body. We may feel disturbed before we can even name what the unmet need is, and if we don't realize this is going on, we will leap to a solution before we even explore the need. This is why it takes training to slow this process down and learn to focus our awareness on the feeling and wait until we can identify the need that is demanding attention. When we can do this, we will find that needs are universal, and in most cases not threatening to the other person. They can be an opportunity to understand the other person and ourselves more honestly and carefully than when we stay engaged in arguing over solutions.

> **Needs are a sensing that something we perceive as necessary is missing. They first arise as a feeling, an upset in the homeostasis of our body.**

Some predictable, universal needs are for respect, safety, self-expression, belonging, attention, and freedom. When needs are met, they go away. When Gandhi talked about aligning with the "Truth-force" and someone asked him what he meant by "truth," his response was "that which meets the most human needs." For Gandhi, meeting universal human needs was the basis of peace. So our needs are central to our well-being and central to any conflict in which we find ourselves engaged. When we know the importance of needs, and when we see the effectiveness of addressing them to resolve conflict, we will become motivated to be skillful at listening for needs behind the solutions in any argument.

Abraham Maslow taught about the hierarchy of needs. He stressed that fundamental needs for physical survival—food and shelter—will always be more urgent than other needs. When those needs are met, we can move on to meeting our needs for security, social belonging, self-esteem, and, finally, self-actualization, in that order of necessity. Maslow taught that all behavior is meeting a need, and that if we succeed in meeting our essential needs, we will be more tolerant of the needs of others. If we are not successful and feel frustrated by an unmet need, we will be more intolerant of others wanting to meet their needs. We all want the safety and support of community to help us in meeting our needs. It is when someone with more power is doing something to thwart our success that we have conflict.

We have already learned in "the Dance" how to support the other person to stay in the interaction with us, by listening for their feelings and watching for their nod. Now we are going to learn *to listen for both their feelings and their needs, and again watch for the nod that tells us we are accurate and they feel understood.* So in the case of the bedtime, their solution was to avoid getting ready for bed and mine was to yell and chase and threaten in an attempt to stay in control. The degree of their resistance equaled the degree of my force—a familiar dynamic in any argument.

In the first step of the Negotiation Skill, we want to reframe the conflict away from the win/lose solutions and onto identifying the needs of each party. In the bedtime scenario with my kids:

> Their need was to have choice about when they had to go to bed. They were feeling mad because they weren't tired, and their need to continue playing was being thwarted.

> My need was to have some time off to do personal things. I was feeling frustrated because I was not succeeding in settling them down so I could get to meeting my own needs.

We achieve cooperation by accurately naming the needs and feelings of both parties.

As long as we stayed in the right/wrong battle of "minding your mother," the conflict was sure to continue. When I was able to name their needs, and put my needs right next to theirs, all the judgments and "power-over" I was exerting were no longer relevant. It was relatively easy to find a solution together—cooperating in creating change and ending conflict—that met both of our needs. They would get into bed, supplied with whatever they wanted to keep them occupied. They could stay awake as long as they wanted, but no feet could touch the floor. I was off-duty, and would provide no services. It worked for all of us, and the power struggle disappeared.

This story illustrates how we want to proceed when situations are tougher than bedtime and the stakes are higher. Using conscious communication skills gives you the feeling of confidence that a solution can be found as you cooperate with the other in reaching the goal.

We achieve cooperation by accurately naming the needs and feelings of both parties.

When the other person's nod indicates that his needs have been understood, and we have also named ours, the first step of the negotiation skill is completed. This is the hardest step; the others will feel like a downhill ride because we have succeeded in creating cooperation. The remaining five steps have a logical progression that is important, but they are familiar and not difficult to do. Now we are ready to see if the other person will follow us into a process of exploring possible solutions.

Step Two: Exploring Options While Holding the Other's Best Interest at Heart

It is when trust is not present, or the needs are so diverse that both parties feel threatened by the difference, that a skill is going to be essential to success.

Of course we are eager to find a solution that will alleviate the tension we are feeling. If we have accurately named both needs, we are likely to float a possible solution that would meet both of those needs, the other person agrees, and the problem is solved. Often this works, especially where there is already trust in the relationship. We know there is caring, and both feel a strong desire to solve the problem.

It is when that trust is not present, or the needs are so diverse that both parties feel threatened by the difference, that a skill is going to be essential to success. Solving this problem is not going to be quick or easy. We want a process we feel okay about being in for a while, and one we know will help continue to build the trust we began to build in the first step.

We want to begin exploring possibilities, but first we need a ground rule: *no evaluating*. When someone throws out a suggestion, and they hear back, "That won't work," they will feel discouraged and want to leave the interaction. It doesn't feel safe. They are afraid of being talked into a solution they don't want. We want to be sure to focus the process away from what won't work, and focus instead on the creative process of entertaining whatever solutions are offered.

Strategy and skill become like a compass for navigating toward our destination when the winds are blowing us slightly off course.

Because we have a six-step strategy, we know that we will have a time later when we can eliminate any suggestions we don't want, so this leaves us free to support the creative process by not objecting when the other person suggests something we don't like. It's just time to breathe, and model for them that we trust the process. I like to use the phrase:

"That's a possible solution. Let's think of some more."

When the other person sees us leave their favorite solution on the list, they become less afraid that they are just being set up somehow to once again do things our way. We know we can do that sincerely, because they are also going to have a chance to do away with any solutions they don't want to agree to. *We both feel safe in this process* and we trust the skills to be fair. Knowing that the skills do respect the other person can make us less afraid to enter into conflict. Having skills that regard the well being of both parties can increase our self-esteem. We know we are going to be okay, and we know the other person is going to be okay, too. That is a good feeling, and it is the basis for trusting that *conflict can improve relationships*, because a solution is going to be found that meets the most needs of the parties involved.

Step Three: Evaluating Possible Solutions

One teacher-in-training asked: "Why do we teach this complicated process? I never actually do this with anyone." I was a bit surprised. When I thought about it, I realized it is lengthy, and I too often just float a suggestion and with some luck (and intuition) it flies. This success is often a function of the quality of the relationship or degree of trust present. It is helpful to know a useful process that we can trust which gives us a way forward when our initial attempts to resolve something have failed. In answering her, I thought of the student who said:

> *"These skills are too hard. I just want to be myself."*

My answer to him was,

> *"Fine, be yourself as long as that works. These skills are for when being yourself doesn't get you where you want to go with another person."*

In this third step, we have an opportunity *to bring leadership to conflict.* We will ask the other person to *eliminate any solutions on the list that he or she cannot agree to.* This is such a turn-around from the typical question of, "Which one do you like?" This is another point where strategy (what to do) and skill (how to do it) combine in a powerful way. If we go with the typical question of, "Which do you like?" and the other person chooses something we can't live with, we are back at the beginning of the process again, with a win/lose dynamic. Instead, we begin to eliminate any suggestions to which either of us *objects. Knowing we have this third step is what has allowed us to be totally open to exploring all options in the previous step.* Now we are grounding the process in what is truly possible between these two parties. We are building on the cooperation created in step two, and we are increasing the safety for each person by reducing the list to acceptable alternatives.

Step Four: Choosing the Elegant Solution

What we now have is a list of possible solutions about which we both feel okay. We have eliminated the conflict by eliminating solutions with which either one of us could not agree. We have undoubtedly both seen our favorite solution eliminated by the other—of course, because that was the origin of the conflict to begin with! This list is now a list of *workable solutions,* because both parties can live with them. The choice of which one to implement is now one of preference. I call it *the elegant solution,* because it has weathered the storm, and it is born of the cooperation between the parties. Often, the parties will decide to

> *I call it the elegant solution, because it has weathered the storm, and it is born of the cooperation between the parties.*

combine more than one and make a composite solution. Or they may use one as a fallback if they aren't able to accomplish their first choice.

Occasionally, it does happen that, in the heat of differences, all the possible solutions are crossed off by one or the other parties. This is a dangerous time. We could begin to question whether either party is sincere in their desire to cooperate. At this point, it is hard work to see this dilemma as about needs rather than judgments (i.e., he doesn't really care about my needs or about solving this problem.) If all the solutions are eliminated, our job is to ask if we really understood the original needs accurately--or if, in fact, the needs have changed in the midst of the process. Can we suspend judgment, and go back to the beginning with the dance of identifying needs and feelings, until we succeed at creating understanding?

Step Five: Putting It Into Action

What makes the difference between a promise and an agreement is *accountability*. We want to be very specific about <u>who is going to do what, by when</u>, because in the next step we are going *to set a time to check in* and see if the problem was solved. So many times we think we have an agreement because we had a conversation, and only later we find that the other person remembered it differently. You thought she was going to call you, and she thought you were going to call her. Aarrg! We want to have accountability accurately connected to what we specifically agreed to do. Following through is a way of caring about the relationship.

> *When agreements are not kept, this does not mean those involved were irresponsible or bad; it means important needs were not being met.*

Something I remember thirty years later from my first PET class is that when agreements are not kept, this does not mean those involved were irresponsible or bad; it means *important needs were not being met*. If we have succeeded in naming each person's important needs at the beginning, and if the solution we have come to actually meets those needs, we are not going to have to worry about whether the parties will follow through on the implementation. Discipline is replaced by cooperation because there is something in it for both people. When we find an agreement is not being implemented, our task is to *re-examine the needs*. We may find that there was a more important need that was not brought out in the first conflict that has now become apparent. Our job is to not blame and criticize the failure, but to remember that *all behavior is meeting a need*, and to once again bring curiosity to what need is being met by not following through with the agreement.

Sometimes people agree to things just to get out of the situation. They aren't invested in the agreement because there isn't anything important at stake for them except getting this person off their back. When we let this happen, we set ourselves up for frustration. I remember wanting to motivate my son Kyle to get the garbage out to the curb in time for the pick-up. That was not an important need of his. I hated the smell and appearance if the garbage sat around for another week. He didn't mind at all. He kept saying he would do it, and I thought the problem was solved. But week after week he would fail to follow through on time. I had to hunt for what would be an important enough need of his to balance with my need. When I framed the problem as my need for help with household chores, and his need for a weekly allowance, we never had any more arguments about failed solutions. He was invested in the solution when it met his need. What a new paradigm that is!

Step Six: Accountability

We want to be sure and *identify a time to check back* to see if our plan worked and if we have the desired outcome that resolves the original conflict. This step reinforces the trust that has been built by the respect for the differences of needs in the previous steps. We may have had an easy time, and the expectation is high that our needs will now be met. But we may have had a tough time, and maybe all we were able to agree on is a next step in exploring possible ways to solve the problem. In the latter case, we want to proceed carefully in order to preserve the trust in the process.

We also want to be able to keep learning as the process unfolds, rather than revert to protecting.

We also want to be able to keep learning as the process unfolds, rather than revert to protecting. If things didn't go as we planned, we want to be curious and get more information about why they went as they did. If we have an agreed upon time to check back to see if the solution was implemented, we aren't left wondering what to do next and we don't give up on the process if the solution was not implemented. We will re-open the exploration of needs and look for a better solution that might succeed. Of course, we will re-set our plan to check back again and see if the new solution did succeed. Relationship is a process, not a goal.

Arnold Mindell teaches that the most important skill in conflict is fluidity. We tend to get attached to our solutions very quickly. When our solution doesn't work, we make judgments that the other person doesn't care or can't be trusted. We need to make room for curiosity and fluidity. When a solution doesn't work, we can ask, "What have I learned?" Something we expected turns out not to be true. Do we become cynical and say, "See, I told you it wouldn't work," or do we go back to the drawing board and investigate the needs again. Most likely, we know a lot more now about the needs than we did when we thought that particular solution would work.

Willingness to address the problem again is central to the Negotiation Skill

We agree to check back to see if the solution worked for both people because we care about the relationship. If it didn't work for them (so they didn't do their part of the bargain), we want to be willing to find a solution that will work for them, too. That is the only solution that will *really* work for us.

My first instructor, back in 1972, had four teenage children. He told us how they had a family meeting every week where they used this negotiation process. Anyone could bring up an issue. The whole family would identify the needs, explore possible solutions, and put the ideas up on a flip chart. Unacceptable solutions were crossed out, and the ones to be implemented were circled with names of those responsible for implementing them. A date was set to check back to see if the problem was solved. The flip chart stayed up on the dining room wall until the date when the plan was checked out. If it was a success, the chart came down. If not, the problem was re-negotiated. They were all practicing accountability and sharing power in deciding what happened. I decided that I wanted to live in a family like that, and this negotiation process was the skill I needed in order to create that way of relating.

Intention Speaks Louder than Words

We can use our new skills imperfectly and still achieve our goals of conscious communication, because our *intentions* are going to communicate more than any words or skills ever could. The intention behind these skills is empowerment; it is to create understanding and to build relationship. Choosing to share power benefits us, as well as the other person, in the end. With these skills, we can have the intention that conflict is an opportunity to improve relationships. We can feel the flexibility of our own intent to learn when trouble arises, and that gives us the confidence to persevere. We have the ability to overcome our own anxiety and think clearly because the skills guide us. We know that if a possible solution fails, we can re-solve the problem because the relationship will be in good shape.

Toddlers Can Do It

There is a video made by a preschool, The Giving Tree, in Gill, Massachusetts (413-863-9218), where negotiation skills are used with three-and four-year-olds. It is thrilling to see a teacher approach two kids who are fighting over a toy, get down on their level, look into their eyes, and simply say in a kind voice,

> *"Looks like we have a problem here. Any ideas about how we can solve it?"*

Because the children have been asked this before, and the teachers have modeled considering alternatives without judging them, the children begin immediately to brainstorm, until they find a solution that works for both of them. The teacher stays firmly (physically) connected in a patient, respectful way until they reach an agreement. She checks back later to see if it worked. Conflict is handled without shame, punishment (even a time-out is considered punishment in this school and is never used), embarrassment, or winners and losers. Lucky kids—they are growing up in an affirming culture that respects their needs, listens to their ideas, and teaches them that they are perfectly capable of solving their conflicts without anyone getting hurt.

Eight-Year-Olds Can Do It

I remember an incident with my eight-year-old son Nathan (who was two when I first started using these skills). I called down from a third-story ladder where I was painting,

> *"Get ready to leave in ten minutes, we have to go pick up your brother at camp."*

> Back came, *"I don't want to go!"*

Now I have a dilemma. I have brushes to clean and things to put away. I did not anticipate this problem. I feel annoyed because I don't have time to think about it. The urge to just insist rises up. But in that moment, while I am puzzling over what to do, Nathan yells back, *"If I find someone to do child care can I stay?"* Now would that meet both of our needs? Yes sir, it would! He went into our communal house, and came back out two minutes later saying, *"Alan's home, Mom. I can stay."* He simply understood that differences are to be solved, not struggled over, and he knew how to do it! I felt grateful.

Teaming Up With Teens

The quality of our relationship was my only ground for negotiating what my needs were.

Two of my most successful stories of meeting the most needs happened with my son Kyle. The first was when he started to go to high school parties. I realized I had no idea when to tell him to come home. My need was not about time; it was about trust. How does one negotiate trust? I realized I had no control over who he was with or what they were doing. The quality of our relationship was my only ground for negotiating what my needs were. So I proposed to Kyle that he tell me when he was coming home, and if he came home then, he could keep telling me when he would come home (he could call up and change the arrangement, as long as he stayed in communication and accountable for his choices). If he did not come home when he said he would, I would have to start telling him when to come home. Kyle had his need for freedom met, and I had my need for accountability. It worked for both of us, and we never had to re-negotiate it, although I had many a late night phone call telling me he was going to stay out later than he had planned. I slept soundly.

The other event was when Kyle, who was on the undefeated football team that was going to a Superbowl, came to me with a request to have the post-game party at our house. This meant half of the high school would be in my house. Resisting the temptation to scream: *"You've got to be kidding!"* I switched into my negotiation gear. His need was to have a place to celebrate with his teammates and friends. My needs were to know that my house would be in one piece and returned to its good order, that the neighbors would not complain, and that the police would not need to be called. Believe me, if we had not had the trusting relationship we had built up over the past four years, I would not have taken this risk. I agreed to provide one keg of beer; they agreed no beer would be brought into the house. The football team became bouncers, stationed at both doors, and all evening they kept checking in with me: *"Is everything all right, Mrs. Boston?"* I felt very respected and supported. My house was like a can of sardines. By 10:30 that night the beer was gone and so was the party. Kyle and I met in the kitchen, kneed-deep in paper cups and potato chip bags. We hugged, gave high-fives, and I went to bed. We had both succeeded in getting our needs met. That event is one of my greatest testimonies to the power of these skills to build trust, respect and relationship based on being heard and having needs met.

At other times, conflicting needs are not accommodated that smoothly. The Negotiation Skill is for when it isn't quick and easy, or there isn't good will, or when trust is still shaky and the stakes are high. Then we want to know how to proceed with great caution, skill, and respect in a challenging process of sharing power when trust is absent. It's scary to think about the importance of influence and persuasion when there isn't good relationship upon which to build. That is why this skill is as much about building good relationships as it is about resolving differences. In a workplace situation, where relationship may not be the priority and the needs of management and staff may be adversarial, this negotiation skill may be essential to even being able to stay in a process together long enough to find a next step. That next step may not solve the problem, but it gets the energy moving, starts to build trust, and the parties *feel* better because something positive is happening. Creativity is opening, and there is a process to which the parties can confidently return when they are ready to take the solution farther.

Fact or Opinion-based Consequences: Why This Again?

Some conflicts involve a decision that must be made—others don't. If we are in a car pool and you are chronically late, I have to make a decision about whether to continue riding with you or not. There are obvious consequences to me because I am late for work.

If you like to watch football every Sunday and I don't, we don't have to make a decision together, unless I want to spend that time doing something else with you. We may have a values difference about whether football is a good pastime, and we don't need to agree on that. But if I want to invite my parents to visit on a Sunday and I want you to participate, we have to make a decision about what to do that is going to involve dealing with our values differences.

When we need to make a decision, we want to use the Negotiation Skill. If the consequences are obvious (fact-based), and the problem is not debatable, this process will be sufficient. If the consequences are not obvious (that is, I just don't like them, such as when you want to watch football while my parents are visiting) then we are going to need an extra set of skills to use before we try to negotiate a solution. We will deal with those skills in the next chapter, which is on values differences.

PUTTING IT INTO ACTION - 5

1.   What are two essential components to identify in a conflict?

2.   What is the difference between needs and solutions? Why is this differnece important?

3.   Why do we distinguish between objective and subjective consequences?

4.   What makes an argument happen? How do we move instead toward sharing power?

5.   What do you tell yourself is true when another is resisting your needs or requests?

SIX

VALUES: DEEPLY ROOTED and BENDING

> *Learning the skills of serenity, respecting differences and, as Scott Peck says, "Protecting each other's solitude" are great challenges to our desire to be in control. How do we gracefully hear a "No" to what we would like, elevate our needs to preferences, and extend our personal support system so we always have options?*

"The more force you use, the less influence you have." - *Gandhi*

How we see things, and what we *feel* is important, and is structured by our whole life experience. So often we assume our way of seeing—our subjective reality—is the way things truly are. It takes another person seeing it differently for us to come to terms with our own perception system. In the picture to the left, do we see an old woman or a young woman? Both are there. If we can only see one, we do not believe someone who sees the other. The challenge for us in a values difference is to be able to see both points of view without judging one as better than the other.

Conditions for a Values Difference: Debatable Consequences

We are now entering the territory where we are upset and the other person is resisting helping us because they do not see that there is any significant motivation to change what they are doing. What is a problem for us is not a problem for them. The consequences we are describing are debatable. They are based on our opinion, not facts. Values differences have to do with what constitutes a "decent level" of such things as noise, cleanliness, politeness, consideration, respect, togetherness, or responsibility. What is a "decent" car, amount of savings, curfew for a teenager, frequency of sex, amount of TV watching, etc? Just naming needs and feelings is not going to generate sufficient persuasion for change to happen. This can be maddening! Conflicts like the following fly up in an instant:

> *"We have to go to church together as a family. It's important to raise the children in a religious community."*
>
> *"I hate church. It never did anything for my life."*

Thud. Her life experience of church was positive; his was negative. She values the nurturing of spiritual community and wants to pass that on to her children. He values spending his time in activities that do something "for his life." Who will decide what happens? Here is another typical values conflict:

> *"Can't we spend more time together?"*
>
> *"We just spent a whole weekend together! Get off my back!"*
>
> *"You were busy that whole time."*
>
> *"I was home, wasn't I?"*

There are important values pressing against each other which are deeply rooted in the soil of what we each know as true.

She values time spent as a couple in a common activity that nurtures the relationship. He perceives that staying home is spending time together. Who is right? This is not a useful question. Where do we go from here? If we defend our point of view, we are in an argument that isn't going to go anywhere. In both cases, the stakes are high. There are important and different values pressing against each other. They are deeply rooted in the soil of what we each know as true. Slowing our own reactions down with nurturing self-talk is going to be very important. It might sound like this:

> *"Breathe...I matter. My self-worth doesn't depend on whether or not this person agrees with me.*
>
> *I'm going to have to do some good listening and understanding in order to explore these differences without arguing.*
>
> *I want to see if I can have some influence, and that is going to be affected by how well I can understand where he is coming from without any judgments about the differences. I want to judge.*
>
> *I'm frustrated and scared that I won't get what I think I need here, but I'm not going to go there because I know it will backfire on me and make him react and defend even more.*
>
> *This is going to take patience and knowing what I'm doing."*

Our assignment is to tolerate the anxiety of not having our subjective reality mirrored, and be willing to allow the differences without reacting like a victim or retaliating with blame and guilt (oh, the temptation...) while defending our value. Can we bend in this wind of difference and

Fluidity is the skill we need now; we have options, we have time. We are practicing an art— the art of persuasion.

anxiety without uprooting? Hopefully, the other person will then stay in the interaction with us, because they will not feel that their opinion or position is threatened. We don't let ourselves be triggered by the differences. Our goal is, once again, to create understanding and build relationship, Our hope of finding a mutually acceptable solution is going to be greatly challenged, because the other person feels no need for change. Their needs are being met by the way things are, and they find our point of view debatable. Fluidity is the skill we need now; we have options, we have time. We are practicing an art—the art of persuasion. The door of change only opens from the inside, and there is no direct route to the goal. In this arena, the smallest modification of positions may be the greatest victory.

Curiosity and Detachment from the Outcome

Because values differences have subjective consequences, they are not going to have the same motivational impact that a conflict of needs does. So a different strategy is required.

The likelihood of resolving values differences depends on the quality of the relationship.

Curiosity requires that we accept the limitations of a values difference, and remember that influence and persuasion are the only goals here.

So we are going to begin with a set of skills that nurtures the relationship, supporting each person to stand their ground and tell the other more about why they see it the way they do. *Curiosity* requires that we accept the limitations of a values difference, and remember that *influence* and *persuasion* are the only goals here. It is also important to be open to being persuaded by the other person's story to modify our own perspective.

"I respond, although I will be changed" is always true if good communication is happening, but it is especially true when inviting another person to explore a values difference. You are going to be asking them to tell you more about why they see it the way they do. You are going to look at the difference through their eyes, and you may feel empathy with their experience. This new feeling may shift your whole perception of the situation.

Our values are the cumulative effect of our total life experience.

They are rooted in important experiences, which may have been wonderful or dreadful. Actually, I believe that our values are more often formed by a painful experience we don't ever want to repeat, such as a parent behaving in a way that we don't ever want to be like, a betrayal by a friend, or a political system we never want to experience again. For this reason, to open to another person's story can be a sacred event; it can take us into their most profound and formative experiences. We need to prepare ourselves by letting go of our attachment to our favorite outcome (come to church with me) and really be open to this possibility:

> **"How can I honor our differences in a way that the other person might also be open to considering alternatives to their favorite outcome?"**

Our attitude of inquiry has to be authentic. It can't be a mask for manipulation. If curiosity is the first important attitude, *detachment from the outcome* is the second.

The Power of Stories: "What Is Your Life Experience?"

We don't ever want to talk someone out of his or her meanings. The greatest truths are best told through stories. *What we want to convey is the truth of our experience, not the truth about a situation.* When we find ourselves in an argument about whether to unwrap presents on Christmas eve or Christmas morning, there are no facts to support our position. If we are skillful, we will skip the argument and head for the stories. When we invite the other person to tell us why they feel so strongly, their story opens up another dimension to our experience. We *feel* what they are experiencing. We *understand* what they are trying to re-create, and then we can feel compassion for why they are holding onto their position with such vehemence. Then we share our story. Stories are never about facts; they are about experiences and the meanings we make from them which are precious. They are the current in the river of life. We don't ever want to talk someone out of his or her meanings. Stories bring awareness; they make space for our differences, gracefully.

> *We don't ever want to talk someone out of his or her meanings.*

"Why Can't You See It My Way?" Church and Golf Collide

A wife believes a family should go to church together on Sundays; her partner has only one day off a week, Sunday, and he wants to play golf and relax. Her belief is not shared. She cannot persuade him to change his value to support hers. There are consequences to her from his choice, but they are not obvious to him; they do not prevent her from going to church with the rest of the family. *They are emotional consequences.* She is unhappy, maybe even angry that a value so important to her is not supported. There are no facts to back her up. The old saying: "A family that prays together stays together" is not a fact; there is very little supporting evidence anymore of something that may have been true fifty years ago. But it is what the family she grew up in believed and lived. That is her story. The meaning she gave it—that churchgoing deepened her family's connection—creates her value today that her family should do the same. His family went to church only on holidays, and the big meal afterwards was the more important part of the family ritual than the church service. This is his story. The meaning he gave to that experience—that going to church was not significant for the family—created his present value.

Values Hierarchy

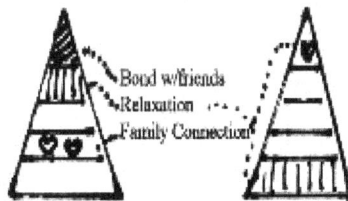

Imagine a triangle, with a ranking of your values that places the most important one at the apex. Because the partner in the above example was not able to persuade her husband to go to church with her, she could easily *interpret* his behavior as not caring about the family, or not being religious. For her, going to church is an expression of her values of faith and devotion to family. This value is at the apex of her triangle *in this particular discussion*. (There may be other circumstances, such as a sick child, where another value, i.e., attending that child at home, would be the apex value.) What is making the conflict is not that he does not value faith or the family, but that relaxing on a Sunday by playing golf is his apex value *in this particular discussion*. Those other values may also be present for him, but they are expressed differently than by going to church. On a Sunday morning, relaxing with friends is at the apex of his values hierarchy. So what is making the conflict is not necessarily that there are not shared values, but that they are not felt in the same relation to other values. There are different values at the apex.

So often in a values difference, our *perception* of what is true structures our emotional reaction (that he doesn't care about faith or the family), and we are suddenly feeling hurt and defensive before we even look at what is happening in our thinking. We become wedded to being right about that other person, out of a defense of our own values, and there is no room for exploring the differences with respect, curiosity, and detachment. Breathe….We have some work to do here.

Options in a Values Difference

So what are her choices?

- She could argue—criticize him, tell him he doesn't care about her, and fight about it every Sunday morning.

- She could give him the silent treatment to punish him for not supporting her, and live in righteous alienation.

- She could leave him because her value is so important it is actually *more* important than the marriage.

- She could accept the difference and "give up," feeling like a victim to his stubbornness.

- She could gracefully accept the difference out of a consideration for his need to relax in a way that suits him on his one day off, not harboring resentment but modifying herself for the sake of the relationship.

- Or she could use the following six skills for exploring a values difference to identify possible solutions that might meet both of their needs!

"Skills Plus" For Exploring Values Differences:

1. Naming the value at the top of each person's values hierarchy

2. Inquiring about their story of why that value is so important, and sharing your own story

3. Checking for assumptions (all values are based on assumptions).

4. Checking for any relevant facts.

5. Asking if either party has heard anything that might modify their position.

6. Either moving on to the Negotiation Skill if a decision needs to be made, or holding the difference (with greater understanding) because it isn't going to be resolved.

Step One: Naming the Values Without Judgment

The golfer is not exactly describing his own values when he says:

> *"No, I won't go to church with you, now quit asking me. You drive me nuts always nagging me about that. Just go yourself if it's so important to you, and leave me alone!"*

Our job is going to be to center ourselves so we are not reacting to his attack, remember that the relationship is the most important focus, and know what skills to reach for in our toolbox to begin communicating about the situation.

How do we name his value when all we have to go on is an attack? Remember that *resistance is information,* not disrespect (a common judgment). He is letting us know—by the vigor of his resistance—that *something is very important to him.* A Reverse I-Message might be the way to begin to de-escalate the frustration before we can open up the exploration of our differences.

> *"I see that when I ask you again about going to church with me you feel aggravated because you really want to just be left alone, and you'd like me to settle for a 'No.'"*

> *"That's right, now can I get back to reading my paper?"*

Since what we want to do is use this difference to improve the relationship, and also open up an exploration of what might be possible given the differences, it is important to contract for a good time to talk, then the other person will be engaged and won't be trying to do something else at the same time. We will need an I-Message to let him know that we are not willing to just leave it where he wants it left, and we'd like something different to be happening. We need to stand our ground:

> *"Honey, when you want to just leave it there, I feel sad and frustrated because I know going to church isn't something you want to do. I'd like to know more about why you feel so strongly about this, and I'd like a chance to tell you more about why I also feel strongly. Would you be willing to find a time to have that conversation with me?"*

> *"Not now. I'm trying to read the paper before I have to pick my golf partner up in half an hour."*

> *"How about when you get home this afternoon?"*

> *"Okay, if it's that important to you."*

Resistance is information, not disrespect.

Subjective Realities and Strangers: "I Don't See What the Problem Is"

Now we have his attention, although reluctantly, because it is not a need of his to do this work. He is caught where so many are, in his own *subjective reality*. He is not feeling any urgency because his need for a relaxed Sunday is being met. He does not see that what he is doing is causing a problem, but rather that her nagging is the problem. He is oblivious to the fact that he is *deciding what happens*, using his power to get what he needs while negating what she needs, and placing her in the fight/flight/submit position. She is the one who needs change, and it is her responsibility to advocate for her value to be equally represented in the lifestyle of the family.

A values conflict is always a shock to a family system. People dwelling in their own subjective reality do not expect differences, and when they happen, the other person is seen as wrong, bad, inconsiderate, selfish, blah, blah, blah. It's so sad. Imagine how our lives could be different if, when trouble arises in the values realm—just as in the needs realm—we could have the same response: "Oh…wow…. we have some work to do here. It's just a little trouble. I know what to do."

Our goal is to persuade the other person to own the problem with us. We will do this by framing the trouble in terms of both people's values.

> *"It seems your value is to have a relaxing Sunday morning, with recreation that you enjoy in a leisurely way."*
>
> *"That's right."* (See the nod? He feels understood. Green light.)
>
> *"And my value is to share our togetherness in our faith and to bring our children up in that tradition."*

Now we have named both people's values, and given their points of view equal importance. We have avoided any judgment that might escalate the antagonism again. We are ready for the next step.

Step Two: Exploring the Life Experiences Underlying Values

Every value has a story. Are we really open to hearing their story about why their difference with us is so important? We may be changed by it!

We want to let the other person go first, so they will feel listened to, safe and understood. We have a strategy; we know we will have a turn when he is finished. We prepare to Active Listen whatever he shares. Why? So he will want to be in the interaction and feel safe sharing vulnerable things about himself. The longer he talks about why he feels as he does, the more we will learn about his values and what other possible solutions (beside his favorite one) might support his values.

"I want to hear why you feel so strongly about playing golf and not going to church. What was your life experience that has made church such a drag for you?"

"Oh, it isn't that I'm against church. It's just that I want to be outside in the air and feel the warm sun. I want to stretch my legs and feel my body when I swing the clubs, to be able to shoot the breeze with a few man friends without it being about work. Sometimes we talk about our lives, our hopes and dreams, our marriages. At times, I really connect with those guys in a way that feels special, and I don't want to lose that connection. I never get to feel that with anyone at work. Can you understand that?"

"So, what is most important to you is that connection. You really treasure it, and want to nurture it. It feeds your soul in a deep way."

"Yes. That's true. I don't think I ever realized that before. I really appreciate you for helping me get in touch with that. I wonder if the other guys feel the same way."

"Well, I'd like a chance to tell you what my experience is, too."

"OK, I'm listening." (Cooperation usually shows up when the other person feels understood.)

"My family always went to church together. I remember this warm feeling with everyone piling into the car, all dressed up, and going somewhere together. Most of the week, we were all off in different places doing our own thing. It was like a party on Sundays. I could look forward to it. I knew I could sit next to my Dad in the pew and just lean against his arm sometimes, and he wouldn't be too busy to be with me. He would sit still that whole hour and just let me be next to him. I long for that feeling of just being together, with nothing more important to do. I miss that so much."

"I had no idea that is what you were missing. I thought you wanted me to be more religious than I really feel. Church was always something I did just to please Mom, and when I grew up, I didn't want to do that anymore. I want to be my own person. I was afraid you were doing the same thing to me that my Mom did."

Step Three: Naming Assumptions and Changing Our Initial Perception

Identifying our own assumptions can be a very liberating experience in conscious communication. *Our arguments are always based on assumptions.* When we bring curiosity to what they are, the rightness of our cause just melts like snow on a warm spring day. Without the rightness of our cause to justify the other needing to change their position, we are left with the quality of the relationship as our only viable means of persuasion. Arnold Mindell calls this "expanding our humanity," when we are able to drop our crusader stance, see the meaning in the other person's story, and change course in mid-stream as we explore our differences. So again, the skill is curiosity, and knowing to ask about assumptions. We share our assumptions first, in order to model vulnerability and show the other person that they are safe from judgment if they own their assumptions.

> *"I can see that I assumed when you didn't want to go to church that you were not sharing the same religious faith I had thought we shared. Now I can see that you are having a deeply spiritual experience with your buddies on the golf course."*

> *"And I can see that I assumed you were trying to manipulate me like my Mom did, for your own purposes, without regard to whether or not it was a good experience for me. I know my reaction was pretty fierce. I guess you were getting what I wish I had been able to say to my Mom."*

Whew! Two good people are unhooking from their own subjective realities, and learning about the reality of the other. There is no conflict between these values; they are just different. When we understand where the other person is coming from, we are usually touched with compassion. This makes it possible to gracefully hold our differences, and even open to exploring how we might honor both values, managing differences that do not go away.

It is a particularly difficult challenge for parents when their children start taking on values that are different from the ones with which they were raised. So much of the teenage rebellion is really about the parents' failure to allow differences within the family about dress, social codes, hairstyles, appropriate times to be home, and a long litany of common rifts over values. Here, right in this tender, vulnerable place, Kahlil Gibran speaks of values differences when he says:

> *"…Your children dwell in the house of tomorrow which you cannot enter, not even in your dreams…" (The Prophet)*

Step Four: Check for any Relevant Facts

It is fascinating to realize that our values are largely just opinions.

In the realm of values, facts are slippery. As we said at the beginning, the consequences in values differences are debatable precisely *because there are no relevant facts*. They may exist, but they rarely hold a candle to the effects of our life experience (and the meaning we made from it) on what values we hold firm to. It is fascinating to realize that our values are largely just opinions. Are there any facts that prove bonding will always happen on the golf course, or with a family sitting together in church? Sometimes there are relevant facts. For instance, when you are talking to a teenager about the importance of birth control, you have a value that they remain unencumbered with responsibility for a child until they finish growing up themselves. They have a value to be "cool," to have peer approval, to be popular. There are relevant facts, such as one million unwanted teenage pregnancies a year, or the percentage of teen mothers on welfare who never get off welfare or finish their education. Do you think these facts will persuade the teen to change their behavior or be responsible with birth control? It's a gamble, it's worth the try; but we can't count on facts to have influence where values are concerned.

Step Five: Modifying Ourselves for the Sake of the Relationship

When the importance of each value is recognized and affirmed, there may be a greater willingness to modify how those needs might be met, for the sake of the relationship.

We started with a conflict over whether the husband would go to church with the family or not. It seemed like a win/lose situation. He was deciding what would happen by refusing to go. She felt like a loser, so she pressed him repeatedly. She didn't want to just accept her value being negated. Then she opened up an exploration of their differences. Now we can see that his value of leisurely recreation was harboring an even deeper need for friendship and spiritual connection that he found only outside of his work environment. For her, what seemed like a value to go to church was harboring a deeper need to feel the togetherness of the family—a need that was once met for her as a child by going to church together. Because in this case they do need to make a decision, this couple can now proceed with using the Negotiation Skill to see if they can find a solution that would address both of their very important values of connection and belonging.

When the importance of each value is recognized and affirmed, there may be a greater willingness to modify *how* those needs might be met, for the sake of the relationship. He may be willing to find another way of connecting with his buddies, like golfing on Sunday afternoon once a month, that would not conflict with church. She may be willing to find another activity besides going to church, where she can re-create that experience of quiet togetherness, like an at-home family night with no TV or phone, or a regular family trip to a favorite place in nature.

With a cooperative attitude, born of feeling understood, many options open up to them. Knowing that her value is recognized and addressed, she will feel differently about piling into the car to go to church with her kids, respecting her husband's need to be with his friends. He may willingly absent himself from golf occasionally to go off to church, because he was persuaded by her story that it really was important to her, and not something she was doing *to* him. When persuasion has happened, when each has allowed themselves to be changed by the other's story, the relationship is stronger, more respectful and more loving. Now they are able to move into the negotiation skill to share power in deciding what happens, with a more compassionate and cooperative attitude towards what needs to be addressed in the solution they will choose. However, sometimes this cooperation does not occur in spite of using the skills.

Step Six: Letting Go for the Sake of Our Own Serenity

What if the husband could not get past his old resistance to his mother that this event triggered? Even if he did hear his partner's story, what if his own fear of being trapped, bored, or controlled was still too overwhelming for him to be able to give any consideration to her values? What if that potent combination of faith/church/family was so strong for her that no other option would generate the same satisfaction that she wanted to feel? For whatever reason, one or both of them are unable to modify their position.

> *It is important to accept the limitations of a relationship without taking it personally.*

While this may seem unfortunate, it is important in the broad scheme of things to be able to accept the limitations of a relationship *without taking it personally*. The other person's position does not mean anything about us. It does not show that he doesn't care. It shows how strong his need is to defend against a perceived manipulation. What are we doing here? We are "aiming our mind" away from interpretation (he doesn't care about me) and judgment (he is selfish). We are letting the other person's resistance tell us information about *him*. For his own reasons, he is either unable or unwilling to respond to her desire to express her values in that way. It doesn't matter. Our assignment is acceptance, and it's a tough one. Why should we accept it? Why should we let go? Isn't he being…(here come the judgments) stubborn, selfish, controlling, and inconsiderate? No, he is showing us what he is capable of offering.

***The only reason to accept what the other is willing
to offer is for our own sanity.***

If we don't accept it, we feel like a victim; we feel crazy, powerless, and enraged (or the opposite—sunk and depressed). Byron Katie, a marvelous teacher of how to discipline the mind, says if we argue with reality, we lose. She says disappointment is created when we want something that simply isn't there. I'm disappointed because you didn't call. The call didn't come. That's reality. I'm arguing with it because it *should* have been there because you had said you would call. It isn't there! Breathe. It is our own subjective reality at work that tries to convince us that *it should be there. We create our own suffering by holding onto a belief that it should be there when it isn't.* Whenever we are feeling powerless, we are holding onto the belief that something more powerful should be happening. When we feel like a victim, we believe that someone should be doing something other than what they are doing.

When we can accept responsibility for our feelings, we can change them. We do this by changing what we believe is true. No, you shouldn't have called, because you didn't. No, that person shouldn't be doing anything different, because he isn't. We may not like what is happening, but that is different than believing it should be different than it is. The lesson here is that we are the creators of our own suffering, and we are also the liberators from it. When we change our mind, it stops. At some point we learn that it is easier and wiser to change our own thinking than to try to change another person's behavior.

Another great teaching on letting go is the Twelve Step Program Serenity Prayer. It is a prayer to restore our sanity, because we really are being out of our mind when we are holding onto something that isn't there. We all do this until it is so painful we can't do it anymore. It's good to know how to get out of suffering when we are finally ready to admit we that we need to. It is a matter of aiming our mind. This prayer is a petition to a higher power (however you may understand that) because, if we were able to just get out of the suffering ourselves, we would. We need help.

"Grant me the serenity to accept the things I cannot change."

"Why won't he come to church with me, what's the big deal?" She is still holding on. The big deal is that he can't or won't, for his own reasons. If we think he should, we are arguing with reality. If we believe he should be capable of better, we create a feeling of being let down, ignored, unsupported. If we accept reality, we are immediately free from those victim feelings. Our sanity is restored. Peace of mind—serenity—follows.

> ***It is easier and wiser to change our own thinking than to try to change another person's behavior.***

"Grant me the courage to change the things I can change,
And the wisdom to know the difference."

I can change my belief from, "He could do better if he wanted to" into "This is the best he can do." When we change what we choose to believe, we can change our feeling from resentment to acceptance. Acceptance does not mean tolerating. We may decide that how this person treats us is unacceptable, but that is about us and what we need, not about the other person. We are at choice about whether we continue to tolerate how they treat us, but it is no longer about trying to change them. We will finally make this change of responsibility from them to us simply because *it feels better.* We want to be happy more than we want to be "right." We want to get on with meeting our needs by our own efforts, and not be dependent on someone else's capability to respond to us. Happiness is an inside job!

To do this, we have to accept full responsibility for our own happiness. We have to be living in a healthy relationship with ourselves, valuing what is important to us and being creative about finding options for supporting our values when our first choice isn't available. When we temporarily forget all this wisdom and find ourselves back in a pity party, it feels good to reach once more into the tool box and know there is something there to guide us to home base again. That is *our* work.

Bless the messengers who come
in daytime, in dreamtime,
who awaken the aching
we hold within us,
who finger the wounds
unspoken and named,
who offer the balm
that comforts and quickens.
Bless them for blessing
the emptiness in us
where stones will not satisfy
our restless hunger,
where shallow waters will not slake
our relentless thirst,
where all of our longings
cry out for welcome
and all that we dream of
beckons us on.   - Jan Richardson
                      from *Wisdom's Path*

PUTTING IT INTO ACTION - 6

1.   What are the indicators that a conflict is a values difference?

2.   Why is it less likely that we will be able to change the other person's perspective in a values difference?

3.   What can you do when you know you are right and someone is disagreeing?

4.   Why is the concept of a values hierarchy useful in exploring values differences?

5.   Can you identify the unnamed values of both parties in this conflict:

> *"Why can't you just call if you are going to be this late? I don't like sitting around waiting for you this long".*

> *"I'm sorry, dear, I was at an important meeting that ran late, and I guess I lost track of the time."*

6.   Can you identify some assumptions they might each be making?

7.   If you were a party in the above conflict, what would you do next, after identifying the conflicting values?

8.   How would you initiate communication with someone who is avoiding keeping an agreement with you?   Or someone who is not acknowledging that there is a problem?

"Your need to have a conversation about our problems is interfering with my need to pretend they don't exist."

SEVEN

THE TRUTH OF OUR EXPERIENCE

> *Many of the skills we use in values differences are skills for our relationship with ourselves. We use them to stand our ground with what matters most to us, while taking the heat of differences gracefully. Our victory is not dependent upon the outcome, but in how we conduct ourselves. We will explore how freedom relates to loving, requiring our highest degree of personal commitment, stamina and intention to honor separateness.*

"Conflict is at the heart of community." – Michael Meade

> *"The Tao neither denies nor condemns anything."*

We have now gathered a toolbox full of skills and strategies that can create the most possibility of shepherding relationships through trouble, but there are no guarantees. All we can take responsibility for is how we play our hand; we have no control over how others play theirs. I recently came across a poem by Zen master Osho, which concluded with, "The Tao neither denies nor condemns anything." There is a freedom and expansiveness of spirit in that perspective, which I resonate with and long to embody. In the meantime, while my ego wrestles with dissonant realities, the skills of conscious communication support me on the journey. Gandhi spoke of his life as an "experiment with Truth." He saw it as something relative; he believed that "being right" is not useful. He honored the fluidity of his experience as it unfolded, and let Life show him ways of seeing things that he might never have seen if he had already had a made-up mind about Truth. He believed that everyone has a piece of the truth, and no one has all of it. He believed that humility is what can best support us when we find ourselves in contradictions, ambiguities, and loyalties that challenge our independent thinking. How do we allow our values—the most deeply rooted experiences of our lives—to change? And how do we hold true to our own experience when others are resisting, denying, or threatening our values and our attempts at persuasion have failed? These personal challenges are at the heart of every community where our lives are being influenced by others daily.

The Fights That Won't Quit (True and Inherited Values)

When we consider the chronic conflicts in our relationships that circle around and around and never get resolved, we are probably dealing with unexamined values from which we are behaving without even knowing it. For example, one partner continues to argue for years over the other partner's habit of always being fifteen minutes late in leaving to go somewhere together. What's going on here? Obviously, arguing is not bringing about changed behavior. Surprised? Continuing to argue will not bring any new awareness. Remember that resistance is information, but where do we look for the information? Both parties are making assumptions about what is true—it's okay to be late, or it's not—without any investigation of alternatives. They may even be making judgments, such as that one is lazy and irresponsible, and the other is a nag. Sound familiar? Each is saying: *"Why don't you see it my way? Why can't you just be more like me?"*

The same old subjective realities are colliding. If we can bring awareness to this process, and begin to examine the assumptions on which we are acting, we can begin to identify underlying values. Remember, too, that all behavior is meeting a need, which, in this case, may be protecting an important value. Let's shift our focus from the other person's behavior to our own. Welcome home! Once again, we will find that the only people we can really change are ourselves. Why would we want to change? If the chronic bickering about when we leave is enough of a motivation to look within, we may find relief from the strife, a deeper awareness of our self, and more compassion and freedom in the relationship. How do we get there? We need a skill for identifying the difference between an unconscious, inherited value and a conscious, true value.

In the 1960, Sid Simon was teaching values clarification. He developed these questions to help us identify our true values:

1. **Does holding this value enrich your life?**

2. **Is this value something I prize and cherish?**

3. **Is this value chosen freely, after considering alternatives?**

4. **Is it chosen after consideration of the long-term effects of believing or doing this?**

5. **Do you publicly affirm that you do this?**

6. **Is it a regular practice in your life?**

> *If chronic bickering is enough of a motivation to look within, we may find relief from the strife, a deeper awareness of our self, and more compassion and freedom in the relationship.*

When my first teacher asked me to identify such a conflict, I immediately thought of the nightly struggle to get my three little boys bedded down. There was a relentless nightly battle of wills. It always began with pajamas.

"It's time to get ready for bed! Get your pajamas on!"

They would run away. I would yell louder. They would argue. So, I decided to see what would happen if I put it to the test of a true value:

- *Did I prize and cherish wearing pajamas?*
- *Had I considered the long-term effects, or alternatives?*
- *Did I publicly affirm that everyone should wear pajamas?*
- *Did I wear pajamas?*

I came up with "No" every time. So I went home from class to see what would happen if, instead of just acting on my habits about how one gets children to bed, I *listened to them.* Oh, I was so proud of myself and I had quite a surprise in store! When I asked the kids what the problem was with getting ready for bed, they told me they hated getting into pajamas. How can that be? Isn't this normal? But I had my awareness hat on now. I was willing to learn, willing to examine this value. I didn't argue. I asked for their alternatives.

Kazam! They had one. They told me how they hated to have to change out of their pajamas in the morning into cold clothes. I started to listen to the needs under their solutions. I started to think about what my needs were, too.

- My need, it turned out, was to have them out of their dirty clothes and bathed.
- Their need was to not have to deal with cold clothes in the morning.

Their solution was to take off the dirty clothes, bathe, then put their clothes on for the next day and sleep in them. Has anyone stopped breathing? Can children sleep in their clothes? *What are the long-term effects? Have I considered alternatives?* I thought about how their bureau drawers were so tumbled that their clothes were wrinkled anyway. Did their solution meet my needs? Could I let go of my inherited value that cleanliness was equated with *proper* nighttime attire? I did, and the conflict disappeared, just as my teacher said it would. (Well, until my mother-in-law's next visit when she asked me where she might find their pajamas!)

In the conflict about church and golf, the wife had an unexamined, inherited value of the family going to church together. She might have asked the same questions of herself about whether her value was true or inherited and come up with "Yes" to every one. Her value, which was inherited, was also a true value for her. It is the values that we find are *not* true that can help us let go of unnecessary conflict in our lives. The true values are worth taking the heat of conflict in order to explore alternatives to a chronic power struggle. The inherited ones, that actually are not true values anymore (and we don't know it until we examine them), are not worth the trouble they sometimes cause.

It is interesting to ponder the times when we realize that our values have changed. Once an avid Christian, I now find I have become much more interested in spirituality than religion. When did that happen? Was it in the heat of debate, or a quiet turning onto the road not taken? Once I realized that life is all about change, and that fluidity is a skill, I am more curious about what makes change happen. I have taken it as a spiritual practice to examine the values on which I am acting at every important turn in the road. I am no longer on automatic pilot. The very idea of questioning whether a value is true for me, or inherited (unexamined), helps me to humbly inquire into what I am creating by the choices I make. When I think of the long-term effects of how I live—how I spend my money, use my free time, consume and pollute, save or throw away— and I examine alternatives, I begin to realize that everything I do is a choice. Then I become more curious about how and why others see things differently. I appreciate more the Native American tradition of considering the effects of my choices on seven generations.

> **Once I realize that life is all about change, and that fluidity is a skill, I am more curious about what makes change happen.**

Powerlessness as Power: Personal Victory

"In the end, all we have with each other is a relationship." (T. Gordon). Our relationships are our laboratories for how we are:

- Conducting ourselves
- Managing our differentiation
- Taking the heat
- Being in our truth
- Being curious and compassionate
- Holding the other's best interest at heart

We may not achieve the outcome we hope for, in spite of our best efforts and "aiming the mind" discipline. That is not the measure of our success. Victory is in overcoming our own habits of reacting and protecting. Gandhi told his followers,

"Full participation is full victory."

He was not invested in the outcome, but in the consistency of the means and the end. How he and his followers conducted themselves was the focus of his daily practice. When his followers were not in alignment with his values of nonviolence, he would stop the political actions and fast until they resolved their fighting with each other. Because he knew he could not control the outcome, and that he would not resort to violence to try to attain freedom from the British, his personal power was in his integrity and persistence.

Gandhi believed that by holding true to his values in the face of overwhelming superior military power, he would generate a spiritual and political power that would produce change without violence. His focus was internal—on how he was conducting himself—and that created his sense of victory. What seemed like choosing powerlessness was the absence of force, but not the absence of power. He taught that as human beings, simply standing our ground is the most powerful act we can take in a values difference. It creates the most possibility of having influence. This is the way we want to conduct our laboratory of relationships.

Carolyn Myss, in *Anatomy of Spirit*, teaches about how our sense of personal power not only affects our leadership in the world, but also our health. When we are not being true to our deepest values, we stress our inner energy system, which can lead to illness. She says that when we focus on "power targets" outside our self—things or people we are attempting to control—we end up dissipating our vital energy. For addicts, their power target is their drug, which ends up running their lives. "Acquisioners" feel they need to acquire power through their relationship to someone else. In contrast, Myss defines personal power in a way that resonates with our goal of achieving personal victories when things don't go as we would like in our relationships. Personal power is essential to being a leader in our own life. She defines it as having the following attributes:

> *Can our inner authority support us to take the heat of difference, and stay curious about another's piece of the truth without forfeiting our own truth?*

- Awareness— Can we observe what is happening, especially with our belly-consciousness, but also with the others in our environment? What needs and feelings are showing up for consideration, cooperation, or just recognition? What choices do we have as we respond rather than react to what is happening?

- Personal Strength— Can we aim our mind and our intention to bend with the flexibility of the willow in the wind? Can we be rooted in the clarity of our belly-consciousness and the skills of conscious communication so we are not blown over by the actions or words of others?

- Inner Authority — Can we stay in the truth of our experience—what we see, feel, know and want—when confronted with opposition? In what do we put our faith and trust when we hit a hot spot and anxiety arises? Can our inner knowing take the heat of difference, and stay being curious about another's experience and piece of the truth, without forfeiting our own truth?

- Emotional Stamina— Can we stand our ground with resilience, detached from the outcome and therefore free to "not know" what will happen next? Have we got the patience and humility to have an interaction over again to change the outcome? Emotional stamina is rooted in a positive, nurturing internal climate, an affirming relationship with ourself which tells us that our needs, feelings and values matter.

- Boundaries – Are we able to say, *"I see it differently,"* and still stay emotionally connected—caring, open and curious—even when we don't agree? If we can't make healthy boundaries, we will cut-off from those who disagree with us in order to protect our truth. This threatens relationship. Good boundaries are essential to being able to stay close when we disagree.

Personal Victory in Court

In 1975, I was summoned to tax court for refusal to pay the 51% of federal taxes allocated for the military. I was up at 6 a.m. practicing my defense. When the Clerk of Court called my name the judge said, *"She's one of those tax resisters. Just file her brief. Next case!"* Taken by surprise, I knew if I didn't speak up immediately, my chance to stand my ground and express my values would be over. *"Your Honor!"* I stood up right where I was sitting, and began with an I-Message that continued in the "Dance" for twenty minutes.

> *"When you don't call me to the stand, I feel surprised and upset, because I was told that this is the court I was to come to, to state why I was refusing to pay taxes for war. So I'd like a chance to speak."*

Every time I got to the "because I…," I would state one of my reasons for refusing to pay the taxes. Every time I got to "so what I would like is…," I said I didn't want to pay taxes that support weapons of mass destruction that violate international law. No matter what his response was, I Active Listened to him:

"It's frustrating when you want to save time and I want a chance to speak."

"You're annoyed that I'm bringing up issues of conscience when your concern is tax law."

Finally, he pushed his chair back from the bench, threw his head back, and said, *"You're in the wrong court. You need to file your brief with the Third District Court that deals with Constitutional issues."* I thanked him, once again acknowledged how frustrating it must be to have to listen to cases over which he had no jurisdiction, and sat down.

My supporters were amazed. They said the drama in that court room, with our interaction happening about forty feet apart, was more effective in getting my points across than any three minutes on the stand would have been. I realized that at any moment he could have held me in contempt of court, but didn't. How can that be? Was it because I never argued? I kept building relationship with him by Active Listening his experience. Were my requests reasonable, and therefore hard for him to dismiss? I don't know. All I know is that I felt victorious. My awareness of what was happening brought me to my feet. My skills and clarity about where I was going supported me to be both rooted and able to bend in response to the judge's statements. My inner authority held sway. I was presenting the truth of my experience without insisting that I had the Truth, and was able to sit in the fire of our differences without arguing or attacking. I created understanding by addressing my issues *and* acknowledging the judge's issues.

When the other court decided against me without even giving me a hearing, and the government seized the money from my bank account, I was still left with the experience of victory—not over them, but over my own fear of losing, of being humiliated or punished. My inner authority, strength, and emotional stamina grew. My trust in the skills of conscious communication grew. I knew these skills would take me anywhere I wanted or needed to go.

Personal Victory in the Family

Another time I experienced a personal victory was with a relative in an estate dispute. Very secretive and (to me) unfair events had transpired, which radically affected the distribution of assets. I was very reluctant to address the situation, since I had experienced verbal abuse from this person on many occasions. I knew he did not share any intention to respect relationships or fairness. I would sit by the phone and think, *"Why should I call him? He won't ever give me anything. He has never cared about me. What's in this for me?"*

Thank goodness for the skills. I knew that calling him wasn't about the money. It was about my relationship with myself. If I didn't call, I would be cooperating with having, in effect, been disappeared from the family. I would be safe, but that was all. I thought of Gandhi, who dismissed being right or using force as defenses because he wanted to have influence. He knew that the more force one uses, the less influence he has. Gandhi also detached from the outcome. He didn't care how long it would take to persuade the British to let go of their control. He focused his personal power in the ways that would have the most influence, with strength, emotional stamina, and inner authority.

"Full participation is full victory," he told his followers. *"Just align with the Truth-force and you need no other defense."* My truth was that I was in the family and I did deserve a fair share of the inheritance. If I believed that, I was going to have to stand my ground and take the heat in order to be *true to myself.* I was going to have to participate in what was happening.

So, into the lion's den I went. I called him. All the abuse I expected was there, but I was ready. I used my I-Message:

> *"When I heard that you had sold the house, I was surprised because I assumed I would be included in that, so I'd like to understand why you didn't let me know, and I'd like my share."*

I Active Listened every response he made—he was mad, annoyed, frustrated, surprised—and then I used what he had just said as the beginning of my next I-Message. I was "dancing" with him. He must have *felt* it, because he stayed on the phone with me for forty minutes even though he could have hung up at any moment. In the end, he said, *"I'll think about it."*

He never did give me any money, but I had won a personal victory over my fear of his abuse and my fear of being excluded from the family. I had participated fully in what was happening. Gradually, over time, my relationship with this person has also changed. I am no longer afraid of him, and I have really let go of needing anything from him. Our connection has softened and opened. Feeling the support of the rest of the

> *Gandhi dismissed being right or using force as defenses because he wanted to have influence.*

family was a much more gratifying outcome than receiving any money, and it may never have happened if I had not been willing to step into that arena of a tangled past, with skills to support me.

I like the lines in "Comes the Dawn" by Veronica A. Shoffstall:

> *"And you begin to accept your defeats with your head up and your eyes open, with the grace of a woman or man, not the grief of a child. You learn that you really can endure, that you really are strong, and you really do have worth."*

No one else can give this to us. When we give it to ourselves, no one can take it away. It is a personal victory over our own fear that we won't be able to prevail, or that we aren't lovable. *Home, sweet home, is inside of us.*

COMES THE DAWN

by Veronica A. Shoffstall
Published at age19 in her college yearbook

After a while you learn the subtle difference
Between holding a hand and chaining a soul,
And you learn that love doesn't mean security.
And you begin to learn that kisses aren't contracts,
And presents aren't promises.
And you begin to accept your defeats
With your head up and your eyes open,
With the grace of a woman or man,
Not the grief of a child.
And you learn to build all your roads on today,
Because tomorrow's ground is too uncertain,
And futures have a way of falling down in mid-flight.
After a while, you learn that even sunshine burns if you
get too much.
So you plant your own garden, and decorate your own soul,
Instead of waiting for someone to bring you flowers.
And you learn that you really can endure,
That you really are strong.
And you really do have worth.
And you learn and learn
With every goodbye, you learn.

PUTTING IT INTO ACTION- 7

1. How do you know if a value you are defending is a true or inherited value? What difference does it make?

2. What are some important things to remember about the other person when you are in a values difference with them?

3. What personal strategies will be important in how you conduct yourself?

4. Under what circumstances would you decide to accept that the other person will not help you solve this problem, let go and seek other ways of meeting your needs? What do you have to face in yourself in order to do this?

5. What is a personal victory, and why is it important as a communication skill?

EIGHT

CONSCIOUS POWER: CHOOSING
A NON-NEGOTIABLE STAND

> *Sometimes a value, a prior agreement, a role with obligations to a third party, or an overwhelming need cause us to reach a bottom line. We are not willing to negotiate what will happen next. There may be strong negative consequences for those affected by our choice. We will learn how to minimize this negative effect.*

As a young parent taking this training, one of the most influential things that I learned was that it really was okay to "blow it." In spite of our best efforts to use these conscious communication skills, we all have those "end of the line" moments when our needs override all other considerations. Ah, breathe; it's a time to welcome our imperfections.

Even when we know how awful it feels to have power used over us, we are still going to choose to do it when we perceive there to be intolerable consequences if we don't. The difference—and it makes all the difference—is that now we are going to learn to do it consciously, so we can minimize the damage to the relationship.

It is radical to realize that using our power to meet our needs at someone else's expense is a *choice*. When it is done with awareness, however, we can accept responsibility for the negative consequences to others, and be accountable in our relationship with them. When we understand the dynamics of power—who decides what happens—we can empathize with those who are being left out of the decision-making. Instead of scolding them for their reaction, we learn to predict and accept their reaction. We would want to resist, too, if the shoe were on the other foot!

Why on Earth Would We Refuse to Negotiate?

Parents often have to exercise adult judgment to prevent
children from doing something they really want to do
because it is unsafe, will destroy property, will hurt
another person, or will create a bigger problem.
Sometimes parents need children to keep to an
adult timetable that they do not understand. It isn't the
child's agenda to get to a dentist appointment on time.

In peer relationships, the choice to act on our own needs or values
without considering the other's can precipitate extreme reactions such
as divorce, firing an employee, or quitting a job. Sometimes our job
descriptions require us to make decisions that hurt other people, such
as layoffs, delegation of work to one person rather than to another, or
budget cuts. While these look like ordinary problems on paper, the
human experience of them can be fraught with pain, loss, humiliation,
shame, and abandonment. When we feel powerless, it provokes rage
and reactions that are often retaliatory.

It is a big assignment to work with these reactions *with awareness*, so we
don't get triggered into reacting to others' reactions, thus finding
ourselves once more in the old familiar power struggle.

"My Belly Made Me Do It"

How different it would be if we came to these choices with an awareness
of their consequences to others, an acknowledgment of our accountability
for these consequences, and an addressing of the needs and feelings of the
aggrieved party in such a way that the relationship was not harmed in the
process. We begin by being clear with ourselves about why we are
making this choice. We are not willing to share power in deciding what
happens because of:

- Consequences that are intolerable, i.e. our budget wouldn't be
  sufficient for more essential things.

- Values that would be violated: *"I won't pay that bill because
  I did not receive the services for which I am asked to pay."*

- Different goals: *"I want a marriage that is mutually
  supportive, and this one is not."*

- Life experience that gives us different criteria from the other
  person's for making decisions: *"No, you can't go out with
  that sixteen-year-old boy. You're only twelve."*

Then we listen to our belly. It's rumbling loudly. We consider our options, and we know that the *truth of our experience* is that our needs are so important that they override consideration of the other person's need in this particular situation. We know we will have to "take the heat" of their objection. We are prepared to meet them there, because we have the skills needed to think well about them even while we are saying *"No"* to what they need or want.

If we don't have a sense of inner authority and a strong relationship with ourselves, we may become afraid of the consequences of standing our ground. Then we may:

- Forfeit our relationship with ourselves in order to please (keep our attachment to) the other person. Then we are not being true to ourselves.

- Be afraid to "take the heat" that would surely come if we told the truth, stood our ground, and made a boundary that prevents the other person's power from derailing something that is of great importance to us.

- Hide our strength; go along with something we don't want, and tell sad, victim stories about our lives.

- Believe that we don't have a choice, because the consequences of standing our ground would be overwhelming *to us*. There may be unconscious, painful beliefs forged early in our life, such as *"I have to be the peacemaker or the family will fall apart,"* or *"If I am the cause of trouble I will be abandoned."*

Here is where the "grief of the child" Shoffstall referred to in her poem may be the greatest obstacle to being in our truth. Until we heal those places that paralyze us, we may not be able to utilize the skills of conscious communication when we most need them to protect something vital to us.

"Have a Little Courage - Again!"

It takes courage to tell the truth when there will be hard consequences to others and to us as well. It takes the strength that comes with clarity of purpose and knowledge of how to do it. Having a skill to mitigate the negative consequences will support our self-esteem as we do this hard thing. We want to bring awareness to what we are doing, because we want to nurture the relationship, even though we are choosing to use our power to determine the outcome of a situation.

Skills for a Non-Negotiable Stand:

1. Center with positive self-talk

2. Detach from the outcome

3. Acknowledge and explain our use of power

4. Accept the negative reaction

5. Restore power to the other in some way

6. Plan ahead

Step One: Center with Positive Self Talk

We begin the Non-Negotiable Skill by centering ourselves with breathing, positive self talk, and focusing on opening our heart with compassion for the hurt the other may experience in the process. We have admitted that what we are standing for is about ourselves and the quality of life we are striving to create; it is not about what the other person is doing (someone else might not mind it at all). Our happiness and peace of mind are our responsibility, not a function of how other people are treating us. It sometimes depends on our being able to say *"No"* to what someone else wants us to do. We are moving from the powerless victim who would say:

> *"Why are you doing this to me?"*

to the proactive adult who says:

> *"This situation is intolerable to me. I know this will be hard to hear, and you won't be happy with my decision, but I am going to say 'No' to your request."*

> *Our happiness and peace of mind are our responsibility, not a function of how other people are treating us.*

We tell ourselves we are not bad for seeing, knowing, feeling, and wanting what is true for us. It is okay to define what is safe, valuable, necessary, or respectful for ourselves. This is the *truth of our experience.* No one can take this away without our consent. Two dangers that can threaten our awareness and ability to follow through skillfully are:

> *We are not bad for seeing, knowing, feeling, and wanting what is true for us. It is okay for us to define what is safe, valuable, necessary, or respectful for ourselves.*

- We might believe that what is true for us should be true for others as well (our subjective reality), therefore justifying what we are doing without the need to regard the consequences to the other person

- We don't have the right to want something if it will cause trouble for others (typical female socialization). Feelings of guilt and shame can attack us from within, just when we want to be our most powerful selves.

The following skills are what will support us to have the emotional stamina and clarity of purpose to get through anxious feelings and to stand our ground.

Step Two: Detach from the Outcome, Don't Expect the Other to Cooperate

> *We have to be prepared to tolerate their disappointment, disapproval, rejection, and abandonment of us for treating them this way.*

To succeed in holding our differences without shaming the other, we have to detach from the outcome to the relationship. When adults are being rendered powerless, they often react as a child would, and understandably so. We have to be prepared to tolerate their disappointment, disapproval, rejection, and abandonment of us for treating them this way. Many people forfeit their truth—what they value and want— right at the point where they know what the other's reaction would be and they can't tolerate it. *BREATHE*! This is not easy. In fact, it may be the hardest communication we will ever have to do. When we can be detached from the outcome—that is, we are okay if they are upset—then we are free to act on our truth and create lives that reflect our values.

Step Three: Acknowledge and Explain Our Use of Power

It is important to give the other person *information* about why our need is so important that it merits leaving their feelings and needs out of the equation. Without sufficient information, the other person is sure to advance an argument, challenging our boundary. As in the case of this father:

> *"Sorry, son, I'm not going to lend you any more money, because I didn't receive the last loan repayment in a timely way. This may feel unfair to you, but I don't want to deal with the tension I felt in our relationship when you didn't follow through."*

Do we want to apologize? We are not sorry for our choice, but we may be sorry for the hurt our choice triggers in them. Is this confusing to the other person? If we are sorry, why are we doing it? We want to move beyond the content of the decision, into the feelings being generated, in order to create understanding. This can nurture the relationship right in the midst of threatening it. It is important to remember that we *are not responsible for the other person's feelings*. We are not doing anything personal to them. *We are being true to our own gut feelings about what we need.*

The choice not to trust the son again is about the father's life experiencewho he is, what trust means to him, what he is prepared to risk—and not about the son. Another father might have made a different choice. The father again:

> *"I'm sorry to have to draw this line. I regret that it is necessary, but it is the only choice that makes sense to me given our history."*

> *We are never right about another person, only about what we ourselves are willing to risk.*

Now it is the father's turn to "not take it personally" if the son reacts with fury and retaliation. The son's feelings will be generated by his *interpretation* of what the father is doing—that he is mean, or selfish—not by what his father does. Who is to say that the son hasn't learned his lesson and would do a better job of repayment from now on? *We are never right about another person, only about what we ourselves are willing to risk.* Our choice may seem unfair to them, but necessary to us. We are acknowledging separateness; we have different subjective realities. The son's reality is that he is trustworthy; the father's reality is that the son isn't, in this case. The father's first commitment is to protect himself from being disrespected again. The son would like to be trusted, and he is not going to get that in this situation.

Step Four: Accept the 100% Predictable Negative Reaction

Our choice has put the other in a powerless position where their only options are fight, flight or submission. We may meet non-compliance, tantrums, sulking, or retaliation. Our culture interprets these behaviors as "bad" and "disobedient," when they are all just typical responses to power being used to that person's disadvantage. These behaviors could be seen as those of a healthy ego struggling for some power in the relationship, rather than as disrespect. That person is standing up for himself, resisting being powerless. We want to make space for his feelings, and remember that resistance is information.

> *"Oh, come on, Dad. I'll do better this time, I promise. I really need the money. I don't have any other way of getting this great car that someone else will snap up in a minute if I let it go. You just don't care about what's important to me."*

We want to *empathize* with the other person's experience of losing power in the situation. Our goal is to protect their dignity, and honestly own our responsibility for the consequences to them. This is not a time for arguing about our decision; it is a time for focusing on what they are experiencing. We are willing to see the other person as someone having a problem (being eliminated from having influence on what happens), deserving of our empathy and compassion:

> *"I know this feels unfair. You are very mad about this."*

We want them to feel respected and understood in their negative feelings—not shamed, disregarded or humiliated. This is true for all people of all ages. How many of us grew up hearing:

> *"Stop crying or I'll give you something to cry about!"*

If they need more information, we want to give it without argument or opening up a discussion about options. We are now holding two points of view, but this time without negotiating. We Active Listen their response to the information. We want them to feel fully understood, even in the midst of a disagreement. A Reverse I-message would sound like:

> *"You're mad because you'd really like to get that car and you want me to trust you. You'd like another chance."*

Followed by an I-Message:

> *"When you'd like another chance with a loan, I feel sad because I wish I could trust you, but I'm not willing to. I hope you can find another way to get what you need. I can see this is frustrating and disappointing for you, and it's also painful for me."*

Step Five: Restore Power to the Other

> *Power is a vital force in every relationship. When we hold power in a way that is out of balance, the other person will predictably react by using whatever source of power they have to rebalance it.*

Even while we have decided that we will not negotiate what will happen in the present moment, we can anticipate the dynamics we will now have to deal with. Power is a vital force in every relationship. When we hold power in a way that is out of balance, the other person will predictably react by using whatever source of power s/he has to rebalance it. Why not predict this, and guide the process? Why not be smart about how important it is to restore power to the other person when we have put it out of balance, and help it along so they will want to stay in a relationship with us? Without this mindfulness, we might expect a reaction from the son such as:

> *"Fine, Dad, if that's the kind of father you're going to be, you can forget you ever had a son!"*

He does have the power to damage the relationship, and he may be mad enough to do it. Instead, we can give leadership to mitigating his negative, reactive energy by being pro-active and suggesting another alternative.

> *"I do want to be able to help you get the things you need that you can't afford to buy yourself. I also want to have an honest, trustworthy relationship with you. If you will start today to repay the money you still owe me from the last loan, I would be willing to match that amount as a loan toward the purchase of that car you want. Maybe you can work out a deal with the owner to give you some more time to get the money together."*

Where possible, we want to rebalance the power as soon we can. When parents (and other authority figures) make an unaware assumption that their needs are more important than children's needs; that is *adultism* at work again. It is a form of oppression, just as when any one group with more power uses their power to their own advantage without even acknowledging the cost to other groups. This prerogative is so prescribed in the roles of parent, teacher or boss; it is a huge paradigm shift to raise the question of the need to rebalance power when people in those roles assert their power without negotiating. Can we really be suggesting that authority figures could or should choose to negotiate their power?

> *The process isn't complete until we find a way to re-balance power or mitigate the negative effects on the relationship of what we have done.*

We recognize that part of the function of authority figures is to make final decisions. What we are suggesting in this step of the process is that we give good attention to the long-term effects of leaving stakeholders out of decisions that affect them. When circumstances demand that we exercise that power, we don't want to stop there. The process isn't complete until we find a way to re-balance power or mitigate the *negative effects on the relationship* of what we have done. The potency of this step in the process is that it keeps us aware that for the children (or other stakeholders) their needs are just as important as ours. We can make trade-offs that may balance meeting needs over time, and therefore balance power in the relationship, like:

"I know I'm getting it my way this time, and I owe you one." Or,

"I can't meet your needs in the way you would like, but I can do.."

Bruno Bettleheim, renowned child psychologist, was once asked about bribing a child to go to bed with milk and cookies. His response was, *"Does it work?"* When the parent said yes, he replied, *"Then why call it bribery? Why not call it making a smooth transition from one activity to another?"* That is balancing power in relationships.

Step Six: Plan Ahead

How can we learn from our painful experiences of conflicting needs that cannot be negotiated, so they don't repeat in the future? If we insist on being right, and making the other person wrong in these situations, there is no room to protect the relationship or learn something that will help improve it. Imagine the father saying this:

> *"You never keep your word. I'll never be able to trust you. Don't ever ask me for money again, you no-good liar!"*

OUCH! Doors slam shut on both sides of the relationship. Remember Arnold Mindell's teaching that the only purpose of conflict is to learn, to love, and to grow? We want to use every instance of differences—but especially the big ones that threaten relationship—to:

> **Learn** – *"What could I do to prevent being a victim again? What do I now understand about lending money to my son that I didn't understand before? How can I protect myself from being burned*

again? Has he learned anything about the consequences of not making good on a loan?"

Love – *"How can I hold the other's best interest at heart, and respect their needs and feelings, even while choosing not to meet them?"*

Grow – *"Have I expanded my ability to stand my ground, take the heat, be compassionate when there is trouble, and take responsibility for safety and respect in the process?"*

Planning ahead is a good way to achieve these three goals. It engages the other person in the process of how to improve the relationship, instead of just feeling like a loser in the power struggle. The father could say:

"Son, I'd like us to agree now that you won't ask me for any more loans until you have paid off the last one. Then we could avoid having these painful moments, and we could build trust so it feels good to help you out when you need it. What do you say?"

"I see your point, Dad. I know you're right. I'm sorry I didn't make good on that last loan. I guess I took advantage of you. I won't do that again."

When we are able to hold the other's best interest at heart, and propose solutions that address their long-range needs, we may end up with a relationship that has improved because now an agreement exists that protects both people from being losers. In this case, respect for both people is restored, retaliation is dissolved, and both feel the grace of being given a chance to grow, and to be even closer. This is the gift of conflict that is done with awareness.

Full Circle: Bringing Our Behavior to Choice

We said from the beginning that the goal of conscious communication is to create understanding and bring our own behavior to choice. We have seen that how we conduct ourselves has a great influence on how others treat us, on whether they respond or react. Parents have seen that demanding obedience gets short-term results with long-term damage to the relationship. We have learned that when differences arise, they may involve needs or values, but in *any* case, being "right" about the person or the situation is *not useful.* We have learned to put being right behind us and focus on relating to the person in front of us. We now have a full toolbox with skills for how to accomplish these goals.

In any conflict, we have choices along a continuum *(see chart on "Bringing Behavior to Choice" at the end of this chapter))*. We can:

- *Control* what is happening

- *Negotiate* a solution; or

- *Let go* of influencing the outcome

We can work with a scale of 1-10, in terms of how strongly we feel about what is happening. If we are at a nine or ten, we are not going to negotiate, because the stakes are too high, and our needs are over-riding all other considerations. If we are below a three, we will probably let go, for the sake of our own serenity or peace in the relationship. We may also do this when the likelihood of the other person being willing to negotiate is low; they need to control what is happening and we are feeling powerless. To struggle with them is not worth the tension and strain on the relationship, so we consciously choose to let go. We do this in order to feel better, not to be morally superior. The middle range between four and eight, where negotiation is possible, is where we are learning to extend and expand our possibilities.

As we move in the world with our strategies and skills, here are some important questions to ask ourselves, which sum up the values, intentions and goals of conscious communication:

"How Am I Conducting Myself?"

- I have done my own internal work so my energy is clear.

- I know what I am feeling and needing in a particular situation.

- I can separate my feelings from my thinking. Even though I may be very upset, I can still reach for the tools in my toolbox.

- I am open to hearing what the other person needs and feels.

- I am willing to learn, to truly respond to them, because I know how to do that without giving up my ground.

- I am not threatened by their differences, their shaming, their threats, because my self-esteem is not on the line. I know how to engage them in a process that will address their needs and hold their interest at heart as well as my own.

- I can make this interaction safe for them as well as for me.

- I know how to hold two points of view without making either one wrong or bad.

- I know how to support myself even if I have done something wrong; my security is in being "good enough" and welcoming my own imperfections, not in their approval.

- I know that my freedom to feel what I feel, know what I know, and want what I want depends on not being attached to the outcome, and on bringing curiosity to our differences. I am ready for anything!

A graduate said,

> *"I have a greater ability now to honor myself, to give myself ground to stand on when there's trouble. I can release my self-shame and proclaim my self-worth even when I make mistakes."*

"How Am I Building Relationship?"

In the end, the quality of a relationship will be the greatest determining factor in how any trouble is resolved. Even a solid relationship can feel threatened by conflict. A less solid, or non-existent relationship (as with a stranger whose bumper you scrape in a parking lot) has to be created and nurtured before the other will stay in the interaction long enough to even use the skills for resolution.

> *In the end, the quality of a relationship will be the greatest determining factor in how any trouble is resolved.*

- I know how to keep someone interested in talking further, by paying close attention to and articulating what they are needing and feeling.

- In my strategy I focus on their needs and feelings first, because I know I will assure myself an equal turn later. First, I have to assure that there will be a later.

- I have the ability to allow differences and keep thinking well about the other person. My goal is to create a relationship the other person will feel safe to stay in long enough to solve the problem.

- I know that how I treat someone creates whatever influence I will have as I practice the art of persuasion. A graduate said:

> *"I will not blame others for how I am feeling. I will recognize when another's problems are not my responsibility, and begin to see the other person's needs and perspectives without feeling the need to make them wrong, or try to fix or change them."*

"How Am I Creating Understanding?"

- I expect that most people have an intent to protect when it comes to conflict, and creating a feeling of safety can open up the possibility for learning instead.

- I create safety by understanding their feelings. Feelings are the basis of all communication and are generated by perception, beliefs, and values.

- I am curious about this person. I want to know what they are seeing, feeling, knowing and wanting. I want to perceive their subjective reality.

- I avoid probing questions, unsolicited advice, and other hidden agendas that are meant to make me feel safer, but which increase anxiety and defensiveness in the other.

- When I have a difference, I can state it non-judgmentally with, "I see it differently." I can build a bridge between my experience and the other's, without making either of us wrong or bad. My intent to learn, with humility and curiosity, creates the art of understanding another person.

"How Am I Addressing the Issue?"

Most people start with the issues when conflict arises, and hope for the best. This is unconscious communication. In conscious communication it is the last question, because our success with the issues depends on how we have answered the other three questions:

- Only when people feel safe, understood, and that their input matters do I start to define the problem in terms of the needs or values of each party, and begin to reframe the competing solutions.

- To avoid power struggles and arguments, I have to first know who owns the problem and approach it with skills that bring us both to the place of wanting to own the problem together.

- I am able to represent both points of view and the other feels that she is having influence because her ideas are being included in the discussion. Defensiveness decreases, creativity starts to bubble. Brainstorming becomes fun. Adventure, new ideas, even risks can now be considered.

- I am able to be fluid with the process, moving from I-Message to Active Listening in "the Dance" of exploring our differences without judgment or interpretations.

- I can recognize when we have a conflict of needs that is readily addressed, and when we have a conflict of values which is a more demanding process that may take longer to resolve, or may never resolve.

- I have learned when to let go for the sake of my own serenity, or to leave the relationship because some important value of mine is more important than tolerating our differences.

- I have learned when to take a Non-Negotiable Stand, and how to do that in a way that creates the least harm to the relationship and self-esteem of the other party.

After addressing issues with all the skills of conscious communication, we can feel hopeful about our next step when trouble happens. We can feel in alliance with each other in solving a problem, and know how to restore trust when it has been shaken.

> *"I have learned to be true to myself in conflict, to make boundaries with things I can't control, and to tolerate differences with love instead of anger and judgment."*
> *- a single mother*

CONSCIOUS COMMUNICATION

BRINGING BEHAVIOR TO CHOICE

→ *Continuum* ←

USE POWER/CONTROL	NEGOTIATION	LETTING GO
I DETERMINE THE OUTCOME	I SHARE POWER IN DECIDING WHAT HAPPENS	I YIELD MY PERSONAL POWER
My needs override all other considerations.	Identify needs, feelings and values of each party.	For the relationship & for my own sanity
Listen compassionately to other's frustration at not having influence.	Explore differences, assumptions, relevant facts.	Shift My Inner Attitude: My self-worth is not in the equation.
NO HIDING; acknowledge the other's experience of not getting what they need from me.	Negotiate a mutually agreeable solution.	I have no power to affect the outcome.
	Evaluate at agreed time.	Personal Victory
Compensate by meeting the other's needs over time.	Invest in mutually satisfactory outcome.	I am detached from the outcome.

PUTTING IT INTO ACTION - 8

1.   What ways do you have of regaining your personal power if it is shaken?

2.   How can you tell whether you want to stand your ground and negotiate or let go?

3.   Under what conditions might you take a Non-Negotiable Stand?

4.   What reactions might you see if you choose this stand?

5.   What are some strategies you might use to minimize the effect on a relationship of taking that stand?

ATTITUDE ASSESSMENT

Offered by Amy and Gary Newshore

Instead of reacting (having automatic patterned responses - roadblocks), "catching the ball", or having a "shame attack", we can "take the heat" and manage our anxiety by:

I can say "Oh" - self communication that helps me take the time to identify my own needs and feelings, as well as options.

I can welcome my imperfections if I have made a mistake or misjudgment.

I can remind myself I am worthy and I matter, even if the other is upset with me.

I can remember that my self-worth is not in the equation.

I can listen to the other with the intent to learn, not protect.

I can see differences as "just a little trouble."

I can remember that the basis of all communication is feelings and needs - the two things I look for in a conflict situation.

I can hold two points of view, allowing disagreement without reacting defensively.

I don't have to be "right" when someone disagrees with me.

I can remember that "I know what to do" to help me to stay calm.

I can stand my ground in any situation with "I see it differently."

I can bring curiosity with "help me understand why you see it the way you do."

I hold conflict in positive regard. I know I can use it to improve my relationship with this person.

I want to share power in deciding what happens next.

I can hold the other's best interest at heart even when we are in a conflict.

COMMUNICATING GRACEFULLY AND EFFECTIVELY

SELF-EVALUATION

- Are you able to observe your own process, see what you are doing and change course if it is ineffective?

- Are you willing to talk only about yourself in initiating conflict?

- Can you say what you need/want rather than describe/demand from the other person?

- Are you able to active-listen in the process of argument, creating space to explore a conflict?

- Are you able to open to new possibilities in problem-solving, challenge your own perception, and be changed by the experience/needs of the other?

- Are you able to move beyond your own anger to a place of curiosity, see the good person in the other, and hold their best interests in a conflict without giving away your power to meet your own needs (or caretake them at your own expense)?

- Are you able to return to a situation that went badly and try to improve it, give yourself and/or the other a second chance to express what they need?

- Are you able to be direct with someone you are having a conflict with rather than triangulating with a third person?

- Do you understand the importance of boundaries in creating serenity in your own life, so you are able to say "No" to meet your own needs (thus not projecting your needs onto someone else and then attacking them for not meeting your needs)?

Afterword

With all of these skills, we can become a force for love on the planet. We become able to help others be more loving in difficult situations. We can teach these skills to our children through example. They will then *feel* understood, know how much they matter, and hear that their needs are important, even when we as parents or teachers have different needs that may need to take precedent. They have a chance to grow up unafraid of conflict because they will not be shamed for wanting what they want. Experiencing the changes that come with these skills, both with my own children and with hundreds of families over the years, has been one of the deepest sources of satisfaction I have experienced. Using the skills has taught me what relationships are about, what matters most, and what loving looks and sounds like.

Being a teacher of these skills has connected me with people who want to grow. Meeting them at the spiritual level of how they treat themselves and how they treat others, I get to see them making the choices that shape the course of their lives. Because these skills are hard to integrate, and require a great deal of personal vulnerability, the striving to understand them creates a community of learners. Stories during the first classes are more often about failures to use the skills. We get to laugh at ourselves, go back and try again, and gradually start being able to report successes.

That shift is one of the most powerful transformations I ever witness. I can see by the look in a person's eyes that they have found the key to open their own door to a bigger, more flexible, more loving and accepting humanity. We learn to not be attached to the outcome, and to be fluid like the martial artist who moves around trouble, engaging with it, but not being tumbled by it. This ability brings a new sense of freedom and limitless possibility in relationships. There is always a next step we can take; any interaction is never the end of the story. At some point in every class, as people open up to each other and share how they are applying the skills, the wisdom of the skills begins to teach itself; and I just sit back and watch like a proud grandmother.

Stephen Covey says the door of change only opens from the inside. It is a mystery to me why some people visit these skills and leave empty-handed, and others leave bounding with delight. Those who can allow that door to open, who find the wisdom embedded within the lessons, leave with increased self-esteem, self-confidence, and a sense of empowerment regardless of outcomes. They bring into the world a message of hope, and a way to strengthen families, workplace communities, church fellowships, and every organization they join. They leave with the High Dream of teaching children that they matter and that their power is supported. The next generation may well expect to share power in deciding what happens in their important relationships.

BIBLIOGRAPHY

Bondurant, Joan V. *Conquest of Violence: The Gandhian Philosophy of Conflict* (Berkeley: University of California Press, 1967). A full analysis of Gandhi's strategies, beliefs and values. Many quotes in this course are taken from here.

Bradshaw, John. *Healing the Shame That Binds You.* (Deerfield Beach, FL: Health Communications, Inc., 1988). *The Family: A Revolutionary Way To Self-Discovery* (Deerfield Beach, FL: Health Communications, Inc., 1988) and *Homecoming: Championing Your Inner Child.* The first book helped me understand how healing our shame is fundamental to our effectiveness in the world. Very practical steps for healing. *The Family* is a clear explanation of how the defensive patterns we developed in our first family are dysfunctional in other systems, such as creating new families. *Championing* shows how injuries which happened at specific developmental stages show up as symptoms in adults, and gives practical steps to heal those injuries as we parent our own inner child.

Covey, Stephen R. *The Seven Habits of Highly Effective People.* (New York: Simon & Schuster, 1989). This is an excellent presentation of a progression of effective behaviors that put communication in a context of self-mastery and valuing relationship.

Edelman, Joel and Mary Beth Crain. *The Tao of Negotiation: How You Can Prevent, Resolve and Transcend Conflict in Work and Everyday Life.* (New York: Harper Business, 1993). A true guidebook with lots of do's and don'ts; it explains how it takes only one person to end a conflict: a very relationship-oriented approach to communication skills.

Fisher, Roger and William Ury. *Getting to Yes: Negotiating Agreements without Giving In.* (Boston: Houghton Mifflin Co., 1981). Focus on addressing interests rather than positions; a different language for similar concepts of negotiating needs instead of solutions.

Fritz, Robert. *Creating* and *the Path of Least Resistance.* (New York: Ballantine Books, 1991). These books train you to get out of your head/habits, shoulds and oughts and down into your body, to listen to what gives you pleasure and fulfillment in your life, and to construct your goals and efforts from that place. He teaches, through questioning, how to listen to your deepest self.

Goleman, Daniel. *Emotional Intelligence.* (New York: Bantam, 1995). A book long over-due for a culture which is riveted on productivity and competition. Goleman introduces the life of the heart, and teaches us to listen to its wisdom in the heat of our lives.

Gordon, Thomas. *Parent Effectiveness Training.* (New York: Peter H. Wyden, Inc., 1970), (also *Leader Effectiveness Training*, and *Teacher Effectiveness Training*). These books were the foundation of my training, and many aspects of conscious communication were adapted from Gordon's teachings. www.gordontraining.com

Heider, John. *The Tao of Leadership.* (New York: Bantam Books, 1986). Spirited advice about how to manage differences with patience, dignity and self-esteem, and how to trust in the natural unfolding of our lives, with lessons as the catalyst for growth.

Hendricks, Kathryn and Gay. *The Conscious Heart.* (New York: Bantam Books, 1997). Many personal stories of their learning as a couple around how to face into their differences and work through them: very transparent, vulnerable and compassionate.

Hendrix, Harville. *Getting the Love You Want.* (New York: Harper Perennial, 1990). Hendrix is a master at dissolving resistance, creating empathy and understanding as a pre-requisite for looking at options in a conflict. He also uses a mutual gift-giving method of resolution instead of negotiation, which can be quicker and more nurturing in intimate relationships than our method.

Kauffman, Barry Neil. *Happiness Is a Choice.* (New York: Ballantine Books, 1991). This is a masterpiece about bringing your reactive self under the influence of a mature person committed to peacefulness, openness, and positive living.

Lerner, Harriet Goldhor. *The Dance of Anger.* (New York: Harper's & Row, 1985). A great presentation of the aspects of anger and what is positive and negative about it. The third chapter is a great story of a woman who moves from being in reaction to her mother into becoming assertive, holding good boundaries (while Mom is still upset). I have adapted this example for exploring differentiation.

Mindell, Arnold. *Leader as Martial Artist.* (San Francisco: Harper, 1992) and *Sitting in the Fire.* (Portland: LaoTse Press, 1995). Mindell directs the Process Work Center of Portland, OR, where he offers a five-week training on skills for multi-cultural conflict resolution. He integrates quantum physics, Jungian dream work, Taoism, Shamanism, and body work in his training, and in these books. He has authored many other books as well. He does conflict resolution as "Worldwork" around the world with groups of 300 for six days. For info, call 503-223-8188.www.processwork.com

Missildine, W. Hugh. *Your Inner Child of the Past.* (New York: Simon & Schuster, 1982). How our past influences how we perceive our present relationships, and therefore what partners need to know about their significant other in order to not get "hooked" into playing out the other's unresolved issues with parents.

Myss, Caroline. *Anatomy of the Spirit: The Seven Stages of Power and Healing.* (New York: Random House, 1996). This book presents the body as a spiritual map with specific lessons associated with each of the seven chakras. Myss demonstrates the Body/Mind/Spirit integration, as she shows how to be mindful of the ways our choices and relationships impact our healing.

Paul, Margaret. *Inner Bonding.* (San Francisco: Harper, 1992). She teaches us how to connect with that vulnerable part of our self that will pull us away from our intentions faster than any force outside our self if we do not listen with the intent to learn, rather than the intent to protect. She shows how our personal power is grounded in our relationship with our self.

Psaris, Jett and Marlena Lyons. *Undefended Love.* (California: New Harbinger Publishers, 2000). This is one of the best resources for how to work with your own triggers so they don't run your life. The authors describes how to move toward emotional pain, meet your deepest fears about your self, and bring healing compassion in a way that brings you to your essential self.

Rosenberg, Marshall B. *Nonviolent Communication: A Language of Compassion.* (Del Mar, California: Puddle Dancer Press, 2000). This text stresses the importance of needs and feelings in understanding conflict. Full of many rich examples of how to work with empathy for self and other. Marshall was an important teacher for me.   www.cnvc.org.

Senge, Peter M. *The Fifth Discipline: The Art and Practice of the Learning Organization.* (New York: Doubleday, 1990). Principles of the open system and the learning organization, and the courage it takes to facilitate true communication in working groups.

Shem, Samuel and Janet Surrey. *We Have to Talk.* (Basic Books. New York: 1998.) Gender patterns in communicating, especially working with the "Relational Model" which asks: "What does the 'we' need now?"

Simon, Sidney. *Meeting Yourself Halfway.* "Values Chart." Argus Communications, 1974. Pp. 36-7.

Tannen, Deborah. *You Just Don't Understand.* (New York: William Morrow & Co., 1990). A great explanation of how women do "rapport" talking and men do "report" talking, and how this (and many other patterns she identifies) creates misunderstanding, frustration, and disappointment in communication between the genders.

Tolle, Eckhart. *The Power of Now: A Guide to Spiritual Enlightenment.* (Novato, California: New World Library, 1999). Also *Practicing the Power of Now.* 1999. Magnificent guide to awareness.

Wheatley, Margaret. *Leadership and the New Science.* (San Francisco: Derrett-Koehler Publishers, 1994). Applying quantum physics principles to organizations, Wheatley shows how chaos is a part of the creative process, and how control of information and ideas stifles growth and optimum performance in organizations. She stresses how to be in the "not knowing" time and appreciate its potential.

SANDRA BOSTON MSW, M.Ed

Sandra founded the Conscious Communication Institute after twenty-eight years of teaching communication skills to diverse populations. She began as a licensed instructor in Parent Effectiveness Training (P.E.T.), designed by Thomas Gordon. She later studied with Marshall Rosenberg (Nonviolent Communication Model), Arnold Mindell (Process work and Worldwork), Margaret Paul (Inner Bonding), John Bradshaw and Harville Hendrix among others. She was part of Movement for a New Society for ten years in Philadelphia, where she trained activists from many countries in the skills of conflict resolution. She has led workshops in Canada, Russia, Uganda, and Switzerland as well as across the US. She has a Masters from Princeton Theological Seminary, and in 1985, completed an MSW with training in family therapy.

Sandra directed a Teacher Training program and advanced classes of the Institute until 2005. She now does personnel development consulting for organizations and businesses, and offers shorter trainings in personal growth. She maintains a psychotherapy practice (including by phone) in Greenfield, Ma and can be reached at 43-774-5952 or bostons111@gmail.com.

BOOKS BY SANDRA BOSTON

Aiming Your Mind: Strategies and Skills for Conscious Communication.
145 pages. $18. Please order at www.createspace.com/6252689

Aiming Your Mind: Strategies and Skills for Conscious Communication with Practice Exercises (the student version, 200 pages with additional charts and exercises) $24. Order from www.cewatespace.com

CCI Teacher Training Manual, instructions for teaching each of eight three- hour classes. 150 pages. $50 . Order from Sandra Boston, 15 Abbott St, Greenfield, Ma 01301, checks payable to Sandra Boston.

Out of Bounds: Adventures in Transformation. A memoir. 311 pages. $15 Please order at www.createspace.com/5149857

Soul Song. A collection of poetry and essays. 150 pages. $8.95 Please order at www.createspace.com/5918127

e

OTHER PRODUCTS TO ORDER FROM CC I

Contact Sandra Boston

DVD: "WHAT DO YOU SAY WHEN YOU DON'T AGREE?"– $20
58 Minute workshop led by Sandra Boston with demonstration, lecture and discussion produced by Carlyn Saltman owner of "Your Story Matters."

CD: TRANSFORMING YOUR TRIGGERS -- $18
20 page booklet and 80 min. CD of six-hour workshop by Sandra Boston
on how to support a safe internal environment when challenges to our well-being occur.

CONSCIOUS COMMUNICATION

- Conflict is "just a little trouble." Be prepared with skills to do some work.

- Have the intent to learn from the other's experience.

- *"Oh"* = shift into neutral so you can respond, not react (automatic pilot).

- Content tells us important things like the other's needs, feelings, values and strategies for getting what they want.

- Tell the other what you feel and need so they can listen without becoming defensive.

- Be curious about why someone has done something you don't like, instead of getting mad.

- Give up judgments. Show respect for the other person. You need their cooperation to solve the problem.

- Give up arguing, and say: *"I see it differently."* Keeps the door open for change.

- Work on understanding the other person; then they will stay involved in solving the problem with you *"Do you feel...?"*

- "Take the heat" of differences by using positive self-talk: *"I am a respectful person."*

- Welcome your imperfections when you have made a mistake or forgotten something, so you're not open to shame attacks.

- Speak from the truth of your experience, instead of needing to be right: *"This is how I see it...This is what's true for me..."*

- It's never the end of the story; if things went badly, be willing to go back and do the interaction over again: *"Could I try another approach to our problem?"*

- Curiosity is the best door opener when trouble arises: *"Tell me more about why that's so important to you..."*

- Own your assumptions and ask the other to own theirs. It calms things down.

"The door of change opens only from the inside."
- Stephen Covey

QUOTES FROM RECENT GRADUATES

"Having taken this course twice, I have learned to be true to myself in conflict, to make boundaries with things I can't control, and to tolerate the differences with love instead of anger and judgment."

"This class is a life-changing event, invaluable and necessary for all interactions in relationships."

"This course is fabulous. It has given me the gift of self-empowerment. Previously, I was frozen, coping with anxieties but not addressing the source. I now can evaluate a problem and have a strategy to confront it rather than live with it."

"How validating this course was! Now I see I am not alone and that there really are ways to change."

"This is the most important class I've ever taken...the knowledge was so loaded."

"This class is a life-changing course. I wish I had taken it 10 years ago when it might have changed the course of my marriage. Now I greatly appreciate having these new tools for my own communication to anyone, but especially for new intimate relationships I will enter."

"How amazing it is! It has changed everything about how I communicate with others. I recommend it to everyone. It fits in well with other 12-Step work I've been doing. The tools are excellent for building boundaries, as well as tearing down walls. Thank you!"

"This is a must-take course. It's interactive, experiential and practical—it works. The instructor is very skilled and can not only give principles and tools but can apply them in the situations that people bring to the class, which is every effective in helping us to apply them as well."

"A great way to get in touch with yourself and the world around you. I feel more grounded and in touch with my own needs and feelings, and value these as much as those of others. I matter!"

"Useful for any field of endeavor."